7-24-07

To Ruby —
Best Wishes
and God Bless
Geil E. Butler

Pin a Medal on Me

Geil Evans Butler

Tales Press • Urbana, Illinois

Address inquiries to Tales Press, 2609 North High Cross Road, Urbana, IL 61802.

First Edition, 2000 by Tales Press, Urbana, Illinois

Library of Congress Cataloging-in-Publication Data

Butler, Geil Evans, 1920-
Pin a medal on me / Geil Evans Butler.
p. cm.
ISBN 0-9641423-4-1
1. Japan--Description and travel. I. Title.

DS811 .B85 2000
952.04--dc21

00-053240

Printed in the United States of America

To
Bill and Bonnie
Jeanne and Ed
with fondest memories

S.O.P.*

The Air Force Wife never knows where she is at,
  Her home is wherever he hangs his hat;
She moves every two years to new sets of quarters,
  During said time she births sons and daughters.
She packs to go to the plains of Nebraska–
  Orders are changed—they fly to Alaska.
Her house is a hut with no room for expansion,
  Next maybe a tent or perhaps a big mansion.
She wrangles sawhorses to build themselves beds.
  Makes curtains of target cloth last used for spreads.
And during each move—now, isn't it strange!
  The children catch mumps, the dog gets the mange.
She is barely settled when she must get dressed pretty,
  Go to a party, be charming and witty!
On all kinds of subjects she has to discourse,
  Besides swim, ski, and golf, ride any troop horse;
Learn songs and traditions of the KAYDET Corps
  Memorize details on how he won the war.
He insists on economy, questions every check stub,
  Yet her home must be run like a hotel or club.
For she entertains at all hours, both early and late,
  Any number of guests, be they eighty or eight.
The first of each month there is plenty of cash
  She serves turkey and ham—the last week, it's hash.
She juggles the budget for tropical worsted
  Tho the seams on her outfit have long since been bursted.
Then just as she gets those payments arranged,
  "The house is no good! Regulations have changed."
At an age to retire he's still hale and hearty,
  Fit as a fiddle, the life of the party;
While she's old and haggard, cranky and nervous
  Really a wreck after his years of service.
But thru everything when all's said and done,
  She will still insist that Air Force life's fun.
She's loved every minute and, why goodness grief!
  She'd have been bored half to death with a big merchant chief!
But there's one fancy medal—all airmen wear it,
  Their wives should be given this—the Legion of Merit!

– Author Unknown

* Standard Operating Procedure

PART I

The Trip

1

If I'd only known how to swim, I'd have jumped overboard. But I just lay there, cuddling my little daughter, Bonnie, to keep her from being thrown to the floor, sorely aware of where I was each time I was rolled against the bunk railing as our ship tossed and dipped.

It was November 24, 1954. We were aboard the U.S.N.S. General M.M. Patrick, a military transport ship converted for conveying about 700 servicemen's dependents and 300 Army GIs across the Pacific Ocean. I hadn't been so naive as to expect a government-sponsored voyage to be as glamorous as touted in travel folders. But neither had I expected the first day at sea to be so physically cruel.

The day had started at dawn. After a sleepless night of worrying about how to survive aboard ship for two weeks without any underwear or other essential clothing, I got an early start to try to find someone who would help me locate and return our missing laundry. About thirty minutes before we were to check out, the laundry arrived. There was more than I could pack in my remaining empty luggage, so I had to make a quick trip to the PX and buy another bag.

All dependents scheduled to leave for Japan assembled in the basement at 10:30 a.m. Slacks were the proper dress for the day, and all children under four years of age had to be on "leash" or carried by their mothers. I was much too nervous to even try to count the excited wives, frustrated mothers, crying babies and bewildered children waiting to hear their names called.

When I first heard my name called, I had reached the point where I wasn't really sure I could or wanted to continue this trip and be isolated for two weeks or more on a ship with all these varied strangers, still not knowing what was awaiting us when we reached our destination. My name was called a second time.

Bonnie nudged me. "Mommie, they're calling our names. Aren't we supposed to go now?"

I thought: If I just sit here, I won't have to go.

"Mommie, please. Let's go. I had all those shots! We've gotta go now."

Like a robot on command, I got up and headed for the door. I was loaded down with two medium-sized, cram-packed bags, an overnight bag, and a hat box bulging with clothes and an iron rather than light weight hats. My winter coat was thrown over one shoulder, and my extra large purse was tucked under the other arm. Poor little Bonnie had to carry her winter coat, the make-up kit, a radio and a loaded shopping bag. (Lucky for us the only limitation as to what we could take on board was that we had to be able to carry it ourselves).

Not wanting to set those bags down, I had our check-out card stuck between my teeth so I wouldn't have to dig it out of my purse to show the sergeant. He raised his eyebrows only slightly as he took my card, checked it, and gingerly returned it so I could again grip it with my teeth.

How thankful I was that it was only a short walk to the bus, as my arms felt as though they had become disjointed.

The bus ride to the pier was quite peaceful. The passengers were quiet, and I'm sure everyone was filled with mixed emotions, both of happiness and of relief, with a goodly mixture of nostalgia. Realizing this might be my last glimpse of the United States, I stared out of the window trying to etch every little detail of scenery in my mind so it would remain with me during our sojourn in Japan.

At the port we again loaded ourselves down in preparation for boarding the ship. While standing in line, I noticed the officials were checking passports, orders and shot records. Ours were somewhere in my oversized, overloaded purse. I put down one bag, pushing it along with my foot as the line inched forward, and I frantically dug through my purse. Just as I found and presented my passport, my opened purse started slipping from under my arm. As I tried to grab my purse to keep the contents from spilling all over the ground, I dropped everything else. My ears were burning from embarrassment as I was trying to retrieve all my luggage when rescue arrived in the form of a steward. He picked up most of our luggage and led us aboard ship.

Our assigned cabin was down on E-deck. Seeing a bed, I immediately flopped on it for some much-needed rest. But rest wasn't forthcoming. Two more women and a baby were ushered into our cabin. Shortly afterwards, the rest of the luggage arrived, filling every available space, and a baby crib was yet to be delivered! Something would have to be done.

Fortunately, our cabin mates had previously traveled the high seas and knew what to do. They immediately unpacked and put their clothing away in the available wall lockers and dresser drawers, shoving their empty luggage under the beds. Bonnie and I followed their example. However, there was only one wall locker, about twelve inches wide, and one small dresser drawer left for us. We still had to leave most of our unsorted, hurriedly packed clothing in our luggage.

This inner sanctum that would be our home for the next fourteen days contained four single bunks, double-decked, two on each side. By sitting in a hunched position, I didn't bump my head on the upper bunk. I tried the upper bunk. Same amount of clearance, so I chose the lower bunk. Anyhow, Bonnie was more agile at climbing the ladder than me.

About a yard's width separated our two bunks from the other two, and the baby crib filled this space. This required me to scoot to the foot of my bunk and crawl over the end railing to get out of bed. Wonderful exercise for one's waist and hips! The remainder of the cabin, approximately six feet square, included four small wall lockers and a dresser along one side wall; the other side wall had a small lavatory, one straight wooden chair, and a door leading to a toilet and shower (shared by the occupants of the adjoining cabin); and on the far wall was the door to the hall with the storage racks full of life jackets above the door.

"Now hear this. Now hear this. All hands on deck. We are ready to shove off. Everyone to the top deck." (Or words to that effect.) It was the Navy's first announcement over its intercommunication system. Not sure where to go except up, we followed the crowd until we emerged on the top deck.

A chilly wind was blowing in off the bay, jillions of butterflies were fluttering in my tummy, and I felt like I had duck bumps on my goose pimples. How exciting! Well-wishers waved to us from the pier. An Army band played martial airs while the flag was hoisted. The big cables slithered up over the sides of the ship. Sailors dashed around to their assigned duties.

Creaking in its resistance against being pushed out to sea, the ship started to move; and every whistle and horn aboard ship perforated the air with their varied pitched, ear-splitting sounds. Swinging into, "Smile, Darn You, Smile," the band marched along with us to the end of the pier. My railing companion was the ship's radio operator, and his words—"You know, I've lost count of how many times I've left the States like this, but each time it's a little sad and seems sort of final"—released my unabashed tears.

An authoritative voice boomed over the intercom ordering everyone back to their cabins for a passenger check, after which we had to report to the theater (just down the stairs from our cabin) for orientation. The captain gave us detailed instructions as to what was expected of each: Our children were our individual responsibility to be accompanied by an adult at all times; alerted us to the danger of the heavy doors slamming shut; running on shipboard was prohibited; open decks would be restricted in foul weather; the necessity and importance of practice fire and abandon-ship drills; the schedules and appropriate dress for meals; entertainment available; no fraternization with the troops; etc., etc.

No sooner had we returned to our cabin than the sirens began to wail, indicating our first fire and abandon ship drill. Oh, what a struggle getting on that uncomfortable, bulky life jacket (aptly referred to as "Mae West"), making our arms stick out like a scarecrow's. In that awkward, outlandish position we slowly trudged, single file, up the narrow stairs to the top deck. The ship's population had exploded, and we were pushed and shoved around so that I never did find the lifeboat to which we were assigned.

When the all-clear sounded, I was thoroughly confused and completely lost. We wandered up and down hallways, up and down stairways, going from end to end, top to bottom, with no luck. I lost track of time and, convinced we'd somehow gotten on another ship, I dazedly started following Bonnie. She somehow found our cabin and we stumbled in, hot, tired and embarrassed—still in our life jackets. "... and a little child shall lead them." If only I'd listened to Bonnie sooner.

Exhausted from the regimented activities, I fell into the bunk, hoping for peaceful sleep. Melodious chimes, announcing dinner, penetrated my drowsiness. My nap would have to wait. It was like a decathalon as the five of us hurriedly changed from slacks to prescribed dresses for our first appearance in the dining hall. The serene atmosphere, delicious food and friendly dinner companions renewed our energy, calmed our apprehensions, and we looked forward to our new adventure with enthusiasm.

After the meal we took our first walk out on the open deck. The exercise was invigorating and the fresh air stimulating. Anyhow, I wanted one long, last look at the States. We completely circled the ship, searching every inch of the horizon, but not one bit of land could we see. We had been kept so busy since boarding the ship I didn't get a final glimpse of the United States. How many days were we destined to view that great expanse of nothingness but water?

Too early for retiring, too late for a nap, and with no

scenery to enjoy, we decided to go to the early movie. Bonnie had made friends with a little girl, Cecelia, and wanted to ask her to go with us. We went to their cabin, I introduced myself and asked them both to join us. Cecelia's mother was too exhausted and declined our invitation, but she gave Cecelia permission to accompany us.

Arriving in good time, we found seats near the front so the girls had a good view of the screen. The theater quickly filled with people in a night-on-the-town mood. The old James Cagney movie was so engrossing I forgot where I was, except I was subconsciously aware of the vibration of the motors.

Just as the movie was building to its climax, Cecelia leaned over towards me, "Mrs. Butler, I don't feel so ..." and upchucked right in my lap. I honestly believe that theater couldn't have emptied quicker if someone had yelled "Fire!" The film kept rolling, the poor child kept retching, and I just sat there. I couldn't have been more stunned if I'd been suddenly dropped through the bottom of the boat into ice water.

What should I do? What could I do? Was I supposed to clean up the mess? Oh, how I wished I were anywhere else except right there. I sent Bonnie up for Cecelia's mother while I tried to console Cecelia. Bonnie reported back that Cecelia's mother was also sick and unable to come after her.

After delivering Cecelia to her mother, I noticed Bonnie's eyes were a little bigger than usual, and she seemed to be constantly swallowing. So I gave her a seasick pill and tucked her in the lower bunk with me. It really had been a long, exhausting day, and my mind and body finally succumbed to much-needed sleep.

2

The musical chimes for the first call to breakfast awakened me at 5:30 a.m. I roused Bonnie, and we dressed quietly so as not to disturb our cabin mates and went up on deck for some fresh air before eating. Bonnie still wasn't feeling too well and the smell of food only made her feel worse. She didn't eat and I just had a quick cup of coffee, then we returned to our room.

Our cabin, five decks down, below the waterline, had no porthole and the fresh air ducts weren't working. The two women were seasick and vomiting, and the baby was suffering from diarrhea. The intolerable stench intensified Bonnie's nausea. So back up to the open deck we went.

The cold, brisk wind was carrying in a light salty mist. Bundling ourselves up in wool blankets, we snuggled down into deck chairs as cozy as two bugs in a rug. Bonnie immediately went to sleep. The roll of the ship was more definite up here, and I let myself be rocked to sleep.

A biting cold rain and the ship's lurching awakened me. What a shock when I realized we were the only people on the deck, and a rope was across the doorway. Hastily, I untangled Bonnie from the blankets and we scurried inside. I found out we were on the outer edge of a storm. Most of the decks were closed because of being wet and dangerously slippery (including the one we'd been on). Good heavens! What if I hadn't awakened when I did?

Most everyone on board was seasick—some carrying brown paper bags for an emergency, some leaning over available rails, and some so ill they were actually green. The poor deck hands were mopping everywhere.

The situation in our cabin had only grown worse. No one talked. Bonnie's condition was on the downgrade again, and she was sick intermittently. My only consolation was that I was still okay so I could cleanse her and comfort her.

Bonnie's plight was decidedly more severe the next morning so I took her to the ship's dispensary. Such a conglomeration of ghastly individuals. Poor little babies laying limp in their mother's arms; small tots uncontrollably screaming; moaning, groaning, retching women so ill they had neither applied make-up nor even bothered to comb their hair (some were still in their night clothes), and some trying to lay on the narrow wooden benches.

I'd been told there were two stages of seasickness. First, you get so sick you're afraid you'll die. Then, you get sicker and you're afraid you won't die. From the looks and sounds of the people in that dispensary, I'm sure they were in the second stage.

Our wait was long, and when we finally got in to see a doctor he told us they were short-handed because one doctor and a nurse or two were off duty because of seasickness. When he learned that Bonnie couldn't keep pills down, he gave her some bright red liquid medicine and stressed the importance of regular eating. And, with a twinkle in his eye, he added: "Vomiting is a lot easier if you've got something in your tummy to come up."

After what seemed like hundreds of trips between our cabin and the top deck, it hit me that Bonnie was more ill when we were in our room. When on the top deck, she had little nausea and dozed peacefully. Was it the stench in our room? Could it be a bad case of homesickness? Or was she letting our cabin mates upset her? We were quartered with two Japanese girls, wives of American servicemen. This had caused me some concern at first. Although I'd never voiced an opinion, I wondered if Bonnie had somehow sensed my uneasiness.

Hoping to alleviate at least one possibility, I started explaining to Bonnie (as well as to myself) that for the next few years we would be living in Japan, and if we chose to ignore or avoid the Japanese people, then we may as well have stayed home. Furthermore, there was absolutely nothing we could do about changing cabins and, under the circumstances, we had to make the best of it. To create a little more interest, I suggested we make friends with the girls and start learning as much as we could about Japan and its customs; and what a pleasant surprise that would be for Daddy.

Weakened from being so ill and drowsy from the medication, Bonnie didn't feel up to going to the dining room for dinner. She said she'd stay with the Japanese girls, who ate at a different time. As I had only been snacking or eating in a hurry, I felt like I needed a full meal.

I promised Bonnie I wouldn't be gone long and would bring her something.

Entering the dining room and seeing the decorations made me feel awfully sad and lonely. It was Thanksgiving Day—and I was eating all alone. Bonnie was sick in the cabin; Bill was alone in Japan; and our relatives and friends were back in the States. There was only one other person at my table, a sergeant, sitting at the far end, and he didn't look any more sociable than I felt. I gulped down as much turkey and trimmings as possible in the remaining short time allowed (I'd arrived late and was reprimanded by the dining steward). Then I stuffed my purse and pockets with all the fruit and crackers I could manage without being too obvious.

Bonnie was eagerly awaiting my return. She ate hungrily and said the food tasted good. Sharing some of the morsels with our roommates (who still felt too ill to go to the dining room) served as an "ice-breaker," and we introduced ourselves. Barbara, whose husband had chosen the name for her when she became a US citizen; Chiko (the only pronunciation we could manage from her full Japanese name), and Patricia, her eighteen-month-old baby. Chiko's and Barbara's English was limited. We had difficulty understanding each other and had to do a lot of repeating. Lengthy chatting was just out of the question, so we all retired early.

3

We settled down to the routine life aboard ship as Bonnie's health rapidly improved. To help break the monotony and to make our trip more enjoyable, each day we bravely ventured farther away from our cabin until we could go around and through the ship without getting lost.

We discovered a library–of which we made good use, gradually made friends with a lot of the passengers, and enjoyed a movie almost every afternoon.

We remained on the edge of a storm for four or five days and then it erratically veered into our path. The ship started rolling and careening, making it quite tricky to climb the ladders without falling down. Even by gripping the hand rails, when in the narrow passageways, our feet would slide towards one wall and we'd nearly bang our head against the opposite wall. By synchronizing our steps with the roll of the ship we could proceed in an alternating angular position. But if we got out of step with the rhythm of the ship, our feet would get tangled up and we'd be thrown to the floor or whipped against the wall.

The possibility of being seriously injured concerned me considerably, but we had to go to meals. Even though it took a lot of concentration to move about, I had to peek at the other passengers. They were having as much trouble as we were! This gave me more confidence and I didn't feel like such a country bumpkin. As my diffidence lessened, I could laugh at myself and enjoyed the spectacle of the unrehearsed performance in which all of us had such an active part.

Good news came over the loud speaker that we were to change course and head south to calmer waters. All were ordered to their cabins with instructions to batten down all loose items and to sit on the floor until the course had been changed. Doing exactly as told, we were glad we did. It really got rough for about twenty minutes. Besides rolling from side to side, the ship started tossing up and down, too, making us bounce around like drops of water on a hot griddle.

This relentless bumping, sliding and thumping subsided and we could feel the ship returning to its regular, gentle roll but the all-clear wasn't sounded. Thinking we might still hit some rough spots, we remained seated on the floor. Sometime later a stewardess stopped by to see if we were okay and, surprised to find us still on the floor, assured us the worse was over and we could get up. We felt pretty silly, but at least we could laugh about it.

4

Our meals were delicious. The fresh air enhanced our appetites, and our dinner companions were most enjoyable. A full meal was served for lunch and dinner: Soup or juice, two kinds of meat, a choice of vegetables and salad, with fresh pie for lunch and cake for dinner. For breakfast we had a selection of coffee, juice, sweet rolls, toast, jelly, cereals, eggs, bacon, sausage, pancakes—as much or as little as we wanted.

My normal breakfast for years had been only coffee and toast or a sweet roll, and once in a while, juice and a fried egg. I hadn't had an egg for several weeks. I prefer good, fresh country eggs fried in butter with the white fully cooked by basting rather than turning, leaving the yolk whole and soft. Restaurants just don't fix eggs that way.

One morning I was particularly hungry. I ordered a scrambled egg so the white would be fully cooked. Just minutes before the waiter served my breakfast, the little pregnant girl across the table from me got sick and, remaining at the table and without even turning her head, she grabbed her brown paper bag and got it to her face just in time. (Everyone entering the dining room was given or offered a bag for just such a purpose.) When that plate of scrambled eggs was placed in front of me, my appetite was gone. I couldn't have eaten that scrambled egg if someone had offered me a million dollars!

By lunch time my appetite was back, I'd forgotten the unfortunate episode, and each meal thereafter I was more ravenous. No wonder I gained weight—consuming all that good food, exercising little and sleeping more than normal.

The weather got warmer the farther south we went, the ocean was calm, and we particularly enjoyed our strolls and sunnings on the open decks. The only means we had of keeping track of time was the intercom telling us periodically to turn our watches back one hour. The ship's newspaper reported the news and included a map indicating how many miles we'd traveled and how far we had to go.

A notice came out requesting the name and birthdate of all children. A couple of days later we received the announcement of a big party in honor of all December-born children. Bonnie was elated because her birthday was December 18 and she would be ten years old. She and several of her little friends got dressed up in their prettiest clothes and went to the party.

The party turned out good for me, too. I had previously signed up for a tour of the captain's bridge, and the tour was the same afternoon as the party. Only ten women showed up for the tour. I felt highly honored as the captain himself personally escorted us. He showed us all the technical and complicated navigational instruments used to keep us on course and determine our exact location at all times. He mentioned the fire alarm system and explained that if a fire did start it could be confined to one spot and kept from spreading through the ship. He demonstrated the Navy's signal systems with other ships by use of flags or lights flashing in code. We watched one crewman figure the depth of the ocean by sonar, and another operating the radar system, which at that moment had an aircraft carrier within its range. We went to the bridge to see the carrier, but it was only a speck on the horizon.

The captain pointed out the lifeboats with motors instead of oars and jokingly told us to get one of those in case we did have an emergency. He then invited us to climb on up to a high, small platform. Several declined. I didn't feel particularly brave, but knew it would probably be my only chance to ever do anything like this, and I couldn't let the opportunity slip away.

Although the ocean was smooth, the list of the ship made me feel like I was on top of a flexible flag pole. Instead of being afraid, as I'd expected, I had a weightless sensation as though I were a bird soaring through the skies with the wind gently tugging at my clothes and carelessly rumpling my hair. I thoroughly enjoyed the excursion and returned to my room feeling more secure, knowing that every precautionary measure available had been taken against any calculated emergency.

Bonnie's afternoon had proved as enjoyable to her. She'd seen a special children's move, played a lot of games, and ate birthday cake and ice cream. Then everyone sang "Happy Birthday" to the honored guests.

5

A few days after passing within three hundred miles of the Hawaiian Islands and losing one whole day by crossing the International Date Line, our ship began heading northerly again. Each day became a little cooler and more gloomy as we were catching up with the same old storm. A few of the passengers became seasick again, but most everyone was seaworthy by now and adjusted to the stronger lurching of the ship.

One morning the ocean began pitching the ship about like a pinging ball in a washing machine. All decks and portholes were closed. Loose items had to be battened down. It felt and sounded as though the waves would burst right through the hull. I was a little anxious as it seemed we were in rougher water now than we had been the first time.

The peak of the storm, as far as I was concerned, was during our evening meal. As we entered the dining room, the waiter was pouring water over our table, completely saturating the tablecloth and pad. This seemed very odd to me and I couldn't understand why. Staggering as if we were inebriated, we proceeded to our assigned table and stumbled into our chairs. Waves were beating against the porthole, just to our left immediately above the table, and looked as though they would surely break through. The chairs, constructed of heavy steel tubing, were dancing around like jitterbugs with only two legs touching the floor at the same time. Since they were upholstered in plastic, we had to hang on with both hands to keep from sliding off and to maintain our balance to prevent us from being toppled over.

Soup was the first course and I learned why the table was watered down. It caused a suction that prevented the dishes from sliding all over the table—but it didn't keep the soup from slopping out of the bowls. Needing our hands for eating, we entwined our legs around the chair legs so we wouldn't fall off, grabbed our soup bowls and began tipping them from side to side so we could save the little remaining soup from spilling. There we were, rocking and bouncing around like crazy and not able to eat. We needed another hand! I started giggling, then Bonnie, and one by one the infectious giggling spread around our table and to the other tables. It was like an impromptu rendition of "The Laughing Song."

The waiter, shaking his head in disbelief, showed us how to tip our bowls with one hand and ladle with the other. Regaining our composure, we consumed what little soup was left.

Without any warning, a loud, thundering crash resounded. Fearing a wave had burst through a porthole or lightning had struck somewhere near, my head spun around as on a swivel. There, sprawled on the floor with plates and food scattered all around and on him was one of the waiters. Was it possible that this waiter, who had sailed the seven seas, wasn't any more agile in rough weather than me, an old land-lubber?

Then our waiter, balancing a large loaded tray on one shoulder, slipped on some steak juice as the boat gave another lurch, and he and his tray went flying with our steaks strewn on the floor with the rest of the mess. It was hilarious. Just like watching slapstick comedy from an old silent movie.

Because of the slowness of serving that night, we were allowed more than our usual forty-five minutes for eating. When our steaks finally arrived, they tasted especially delicious, even though we were still struggling to remain on our chairs and had difficulty eating. (Later, we learned that so many trays of food were spilled that evening that those eating after us had only peanut butter sandwiches and canned fruit.)

Having witnessed a baby in a high chair upset with such force he didn't even cry and was rushed to the dispensary, I soberly considered the potential hazards in returning to our cabin. We proceeded with extreme caution, clinging desperately to the foul-weather railings as we inched our way along the narrow passageways and down the three steep ladder-wells until we arrived safely in our cabin. It was early, but there was no movie that night and nothing else to do, so we retired. I wouldn't let Bonnie sleep in the top bunk for fear she'd be tossed out. Although I knew I'd be bruised and sore from being tossed against the bunk railing, I was grateful it confined and prevented us from being thrown to the floor.

Cuddling Bonnie, I tried to soothe away her fears. Maybe I was trying to get rid of some of mine, too. I was remembering my visit to the captain's bridge where I'd seen the instrument that registered the maximum roll of the ship. On our first encounter with this storm the list of the ship had pushed the needle on the indicator to within just a notch or two of the last mark. The captain told us if the ship rolled beyond that point the ship might possibly capsize. A disturbing thought, as it seemed we were in rougher waters now than earlier.

My mind mulled over the probabilities. If the ship did capsize, I would have to strap a bulky "Mae West" life jacket on each of us, push and shove our way through the masses from E-deck to the top deck, and then try to find a lifeboat. But I'd never even seen a lifeboat on either of our fire and abandon ship drills! I was convinced I'd never locate one in a panic-stricken situation. Our chances of survival seemed pretty slim.

My brain felt like it might explode. There were so many things to think about, all so frightening and nothing I could do. I decided right then and there to try to imitate Scarlett O'Hara and kept repeating, "I'll just worry about it all tomorrow," until I finally found solace in sleep.

6

The last few days sent spirits soaring as we began counting the hours and then the minutes until our arrival. Everyone wanted the few washing machines and irons so clothing could be laundered and repacked. Women were scurrying from cabin to cabin trying new hairstyles, deciding on the best outfit in which to meet their husbands, and helping each other in the seemingly impossible task of getting all their belongings repacked. American currency couldn't be used in Japan, and we had to have our money exchanged into Military Pay Script (MPS).

The projected day before arrival in Yokohama, we each received an invitation to the Captain's Dinner. The dining room was decorated with balloons and colored streamers, with soft dinner music in the background; and everyone, dressed in their very best, was in a wonderfully gay and festive mood. Our menu read as though we were dining in any one of the better restaurants of any city of the United States:

Celery En Branche
Stuffed Olives Garden Radishes
Green Onions
Oyster Stew, Saltines
Cocktail: Chilled Fruit Cup
Fresh Crab Meat Salad, 1000 Island Dressing
Grilled Loin Steak
Mushroom Sauce or Garlic Butter
Roast Tom Turkey
Imperial Stuffing, Gravy, Cranberry Sauce
Whipped Potatoes Buttered Green Beans
French Fried Potatoes Buttered Broccoli
Steamed White Rice
Clover Leaf Rolls

Mixed Fruit Compote
Ice Cream Fruit Cake
Fresh Strawberry Shortcake, Whipped Cream
Preserved Purple Plums
Yellow Cling Peaches

- Cheese -
American Swiss Bleu

Coffee Tea Cocoa Fresh Milk
Buttermilk

Fresh Fruit in Season
Assorted Mixed Nuts Assorted Hard Candy

Needless to say, we all ate heartily and loaded down with fruit, nuts, candy and balloons to take back to the cabins. In order to be up and out on deck long before breakfast, three or four hours of sleep was the maximum for any of the women that night by the time showers were taken, heads washed, hair set and all baggage repacked.

Visibility was poor the next morning, and it was a gloomy, foggy day. The faint line of mountains in the far distance was our first sight of land in fifteen days. The intercom was crackling that we were just outside the bay, proceeding at low speed while waiting for the submarine locks to open.

After breakfast we got a good spot on the rail to watch all the activity. The ship just coasted along on entering the bay because of the congestion of so many crafts: fishing boats, sampans, barges, freighters, passenger ships, pilot ships and Navy ships—each flying a flag of a different country. Fascinated as children at a circus, we strained our necks and eyes so we wouldn't miss a single thing.

Excitedly I watched a little Japanese harbor craft coming straight toward us as though it would ram right into the side of the ship. A nearby crew member explained that a Japanese pilot (to pilot our ship), an Army boarding officer (responsible for delivering all the dependents to their sponsors), and a Navy officer (with orders for our ship's master) were on that small boat and would be boarding our ship. Leaning over the railing, we could see the pilot boat pull alongside and watched as the three officers climbed up the side of our ship on a teetering rope ladder lowered for them.

All dependents were ordered to go below to the ship's theater for landing instructions. The boarding officer explained the procedures of customs and clearance, and that as soon as the transport was tied to the pier we must go straight to our cabins, remaining there until our sponsors (husbands) came for us. He answered a few questions, but everyone was most anxious to get topside as soon as possible and weren't particularly interested in what he was saying. He concluded with the statement that he thought all mothers who traveled overseas to join their husbands deserved an award, since he felt most husbands didn't fully realize the trials and tribulations involved in such a trip. If he had his way, he'd take the fathers and children for a ride in the bay, giving the mothers some rest. He believed two hours would be sufficient for our husbands to appreciate a little more of what we'd been through in coming to Japan.

Upon dismissal, there was a mad rush to the top deck. The pushing and shoving to get a rail position was worse than at any bargain sale. Two tugs slowly pushed the transport around into position for docking. A crowd of men, huddled behind a fence, emerged into individuals holding flowers or boxes, and each up-turned face was searching and hoping for recognition. An Army band was loudly welcoming us with its music, and one by one wives and husbands began waving. Then pandemonium broke loose. Yelling, screaming women and boisterous men's voices reverberated all around. Bonnie located her Daddy, but in all that tumult with tears of happiness and relief streaming down my face, I wasn't sure of anything.

Over all that noise the intercom blared out: "Now hear this. Now hear this. All dependents please go below to your cabins. Your sponsors are coming aboard." Reluctantly, we returned to our cabins to wait.

It seemed forever before we heard the first footsteps on our ladder, and Bonnie was so sure it was her Daddy she dashed out of the cabin. It wasn't. To make sure he would find us, we stood in the doorway. With the first glimpse of those coming down and after directing a few men to the right cabins, I knew they were just as excited and befuddled as me. And then came Bill.

Bonnie ran to him and leaped right up into his arms, knocking his hat off, and nearly squashing the two beautiful orchids he was carrying. After a loving kiss and a tight bear hug for each of us, Bill interrupted Bonnie's magpie chattering, saying we should leave right away, if we had everything ready, to avoid being caught in a long line at customs. He had already made arrangements with a Japanese boy to carry our luggage.

How strange it was walking down the gangplank onto solid ground. Not totally aware of the surroundings, I just hung onto Bill's arm and we followed the boy with our luggage. Our passports and luggage were checked through customs, and we made our way on through what seemed like a huge warehouse until we came out onto a street. A government staff car was waiting for us, and the Japanese driver loaded us and our baggage into the car for the two-hour ride to Tokyo.

7

My first vague impression of Yokohama was its similarity to any large, bustling city with tall buildings and heavy traffic. It did seem strange traveling on the left side of the road—and the excessive number of bicycles—and so many people wearing gauze masks over their nose and mouth. Bill explained these were worn due to the prevalence of colds and flu. Instead of looking out the car windows at the strange, foreign countryside, I could only look at Bill. It was like a dream. I felt if I blinked my eyes or let go of his hand, he'd disappear.

His simple question: "How was your trip?" closed the gap of the past six months' separation. Bonnie and I started telling him all that had happened—about selling most of our furniture; collecting the rugs to keep the house warm and getting an electric stove-refrigerator combination; trading our old car for a new 1954 blue and white Chrysler; making arrangements for our house to be rented; finding a good home for Trixie, our five-year-old dog; getting our passports and suffering through fourteen inoculation shots apiece; sorting and packing the remainder of our household goods for storage, to be shipped overseas, hold baggage and cabin baggage; and attending farewell parties and bidding adieus to our friends and relatives who considered us very fortunate in having such a wonderful opportunity.

Bonnie told him all about the dance revue she was in, and I apologized for having to delay our trip so she could be in the revue. I explained to him that when our port call finally arrived about mid-October and I settled down to the serious business of taking care of the last-minute details prior to leaving Rantoul, the enchantment of an ocean voyage started disintegrating and a frightening fact had emerged—that Bonnie and I would be traveling half-way around the world without his physical and moral support.

As the time drew nearer for us to leave, new fears had developed and Japan seemed farther away. After one fitful, flopping night filled with nightmares in which our boat was hanging upside down on the other side of the world and I was jumping from one sampan to another in the middle of the ocean, I was so upset I'd put in the long distance call to tell him I just didn't think I could make the trip. But, being his usual practical self, he'd reminded me that I'd already shipped most of our things and (rather curtly) he thought it was a little late for me to be changing my mind, arguing that most people jumped at such an opportunity, and he knew Bonnie and I both would enjoy the experience. Then (less harshly), he'd said he really wanted and needed us to come to Japan to be with him. The familiarity of his voice and his words of encouragement had been just what I'd needed to dispel the qualms of the last few days, and I told him all about our trip.

My sister and brother-in-law graciously offered to accompany us to the west coast so we wouldn't have the long drive alone. As they had never been through the western part of the United States, we left in sufficient time to have a leisurely vacation trip to Seattle. Although Bill had specifically told me to take the southern route to avoid any risk of getting caught in a snowstorm along the way, the weather had been so beautiful all that fall I disregarded his advice and decided to plan our route day by day.

We left Rantoul, in the east-central part of Illinois, heading southwesterly through St. Louis, and on through Missouri into Kansas. In Kansas we took a short side trip into the country to see a very old sod house that was completely furnished with early settlers' furniture. My sister and I particularly enjoyed this, as our father had been born and lived in Kansas as a boy and we wondered if he'd perhaps lived in just such a place. Then we went on to Colorado, where we had some trouble finding motel accommodations, as many motels had already closed down for the winter season.

The next morning we were surprised to find the ground covered with new fallen snow. but, after breakfast, we optimistically started up the road leading through Rabbit Ears Pass. The first mile or so wasn't too bad, but then the higher we went the slipperier it got. Hank was driving and I was in the front with him. Bonnie and June were in the back seat, and I could literally feel my sister's feet pushing through the front seat whenever we would slip or slide a little. I was getting a little jittery myself, as there were no guard rails and we could look right down into deep ravines.

Finally, we reached a spot in the road where the car refused to go any higher and started slipping more and more to the side of the road and we just had to stop and give up. The road wasn't wide enough to turn the car around, and the thought of just sitting there for possibly hours waiting for the snow to melt wasn't a very consoling thought. We all agreed the only sensible thing to do was to go back from whence we came, if we could just figure out how to do that!

Hank shifted into reverse and very slowly started backing up. He seemed to have pretty good control of the car. At least he was easing us away from the edge of the drop-off and back onto the road. He kept backing quite a ways until we found a place wide enough for him to turn the car around so we could go down the mountain road in the proper manner.

Our mouths were so dry from nervous tension we pulled into a little restaurant for a cup of coffee. As we sipped that hot coffee, we discussed our predicament and tried to decide what we should do. We overheard some truck drivers in the next booth discussing the roads and weather and how clear it was on the other side of the pass. This was encouraging news. So Hank went out and bought some tire chains and had them put on the car. Then, proceeding cautiously and with the help of the bright sunshine melting the snow, we got through the pass. And, just as we'd overheard, the road on the other side of the pass was dry, with no signs of snow anywhere.

In Salt Lake City we spent most of one day touring the Mormon Temple, the grounds and buildings, and we were most impressed by the clean, well-kept premises and the dedication of the Mormon people.

It seemed a waste of time to keep driving due west to the coast and then head north, so I picked out a route that would take us northwesterly through Idaho on into Washington. I'd made a poor choice. The country was very desolate and all we could see for many long, lonesome miles were some wild buffalo, deer and a few stray steers. And, our gas tank was getting low. In the nick of time we found a little service station, completely isolated. The owner and his wife, who lived there, told us they didn't see too many people traveling that road. We had a nice little visit with them; they gave Bonnie an apple, and extended their best wishes for our safe journey. The rest of the trip was uneventful, and we spent the last night on the road in a motel in the outskirts of Seattle.

The embarkation center was typical of most World War II military bases—lots of temporary-type buildings that looked like barracks, except mostly women and children were milling through the buildings and around the grounds. I presented our orders, got checked in and was assigned to a room. Our room, rather small with two army cots and just enough space to store our luggage, was adequate and about what I'd expected.

June and Hank were permitted to spend one night at the hostess house near us. After dinner in the mess hall, we all enjoyed a movie in the Base Theater. However, I didn't sleep as well that night as I had in the motels. Hank took my car to town early the next morning for a last check-up and made their reservations to fly back home that afternoon. June and Bonnie accompanied me as I tried to familiarize myself with the location of the various buildings. And, too soon, it was time to say our tearful good-byes, and I was left on my own.

I had a full schedule of meetings and orientations to attend so as to know what was expected of us. Since several ships would be leaving in the next few days for various places, it was our own individual responsibility to check the bulletin board daily for specific instructions for our particular shipment. With June and Hank gone and Bonnie and I finally on our own, my tremendous responsibility felt like a heavy yoke weighing on my shoulders. Bill had always taken care of all of the details in our previous stateside travels and now, faced with my first overseas trip, even with all those people around, I felt terribly alone and very unsure of myself. My sister's parting words had been: "Don't worry. You'll get along fine. Just remember you're all in the same boat." Well, I guess we would be, provided Bonnie and I just got on the right boat!

During our trip I hadn't bothered about doing any laundry, so I inquired about getting it done. I located the laundry room, but was shocked at the number of women standing in line just to sign up for a later time to use one of the few available washers. Feeling sorry for the ones with babies or several children, I sent our laundry out to a commercial firm rather than deprive someone who needed the facilities worse than I.

A notice was on the bulletin board that cars to be shipped overseas were to be driven to the pier the next morning and no passengers were permitted to accompany the driver. The nursery seemed the logical place to leave Bonnie. Insulted that I considered her "a baby," she argued that a nine-year-old was too big for the nursery and that she'd rather stay in our room alone. Reluctantly, I finally gave in to her.

Worrisome thoughts about leaving Bonnie alone and me driving in a strange city had so interfered with my sleep that I was worn out before I started out that morning. Some of the gals drove like they were in a demolition race as they jockeyed for position. Consequently, I ended up about half-way back of possibly thirty cars lined up single file behind a military truck that was to lead us to the pier.

We rolled right along at a good speed, even when we entered on more heavily traveled streets with traffic signs. We had been told to obey the traffic signals, as we were not considered a convoy. I had such a fear of getting lost that I never once let the car in front of me out of my sight. I don't think I even blinked my eyelids.

Wild thoughts started whirling through my mind: Why hadn't I been smart enough to have learned the route before we left? Do I dare glance away from the car I'm following to at least see the name of the street we're on? No, no, I'd better not risk it ... Oh darn, another traffic signal. Please, please, let me get through it before it turns red ... Boy, I just made it on yellow. We seem to be going fairly fast, maybe the next one won't be so close. I wonder what direction the pier is? How many more miles of this do we have? Whoops! That light turned red before I got through. I'd better watch those traffic lights better, or I'll get a ticket. Then what would happen to me? Or worse, what if I got involved in a wreck? Oh, oh. I can't possibly get through this light . . . Boy, they're going fast. That white car is getting away from me. Hope they don't turn a corner ... Please, don't any of you other people turn and get between me and the white car ... The light's green. Here we go, Geil. ...

The squealing of the tires cleared my mind. I caught up with the car I'd been following (by exceeding the speed limit, I'm sure), and from then on to the pier I stuck so close to that white car I'm sure we appeared to be glued together.

At the pier our orders and cars were checked, we turned over the keys, and boarded a waiting bus. I was so thankful for the safe trip out and, after my sleepless night, I just closed my eyes and tried to relax a little on the return trip. It was such a relief to be back with Bonnie. I don't know which of us was happier.

A bulletin was posted that all hold baggage would be picked up that evening as we were to sail the next day. Excitement was running high for everyone—except me. Unfortunately, our laundry hadn't returned and it included most of our underwear and other essential clothing. The thought of being on shipboard for two weeks or longer without those clothes threw me into a dither. Not knowing what else to do under the circumstances, I half-heartedly repacked all four of our big bags so they could be picked up.

And I talked on and on about our experiences on the ship. Bill listened attentively, interjecting a few "You should have known better's," and "I told you about that's."

"Well, here we are," he said, pointing to a house in front of us. "That's our place."

I could hardly believe that I had been talking to him for almost two solid hours. We had arrived at the place we were to call home for the next two and a half years.

Part II

Settling In and Getting Through the Holidays

8

The place Bill had rented was one of five small, white-frame houses built on a little bluff overlooking the street. Japanese owned, constructed in Western style, they were small compared to American standards but looked good after having been cooped up in a small ship cabin for fifteen days.

Bill and the driver carried in our luggage. I sank down in the nearest chair, let my head roll back and closed my eyes. Oh, how tired I was. The sensation of perpetual movement still in my body unleashed my long suppressed fears, anxieties and loneliness, letting them ooze out leaving me completely spent.

"Mom. Mom. C'mon," Bonnie said, taking my hand and trying to pull me up out of the chair I'd dropped in as soon as I got inside. "Daddy and I want to show you the house."

Willfully forcing some strength back into my muscles and while trying to clear my glazed eyes, I glanced around the room. Bill had completely furnished the place with government-issue furniture. The over-stuffed chair I was sitting in was upholstered in aqua velveteen, one of a matched set cozily arranged at either end of a fake fireplace. Two vases filled with beautiful fresh flowers were on the mantle. The front wall of the living room was sliding glass doors, frosted except for the top ten or twelve inches. Just inside the front door was an old-fashioned kerosene heater, the pipe going out the wall above the door. In the corner near the heater were two adjacent doors which opened into the bedrooms; and about three feet from them in the back wall was a closed door. A small kitchen table, surrounded by four wooden straight chairs, completely filled the small wall space between the closed door and the kitchen door. The room wasn't much larger than our cabin had been, but at least we had some other rooms and Bonnie was impatiently pulling on me to see the rest of the house.

"See, Mom, this is my room," she said and exuberantly jumped on her three-quarter size bed. "And look, I've got my very own flowers." She pointed to a small bouquet of fresh pink roses on a night table that partially blocked the sliding doors to a closet.

The room was small with just enough space to walk around the bed. A small dresser stood under the short, double windows at the foot of the bed, with another small window in the corner of the adjoining wall. Next was our bedroom. It was a little larger than Bonnie's room and had a double bed. Under a short double window at the far end was a chest of drawers, blocking off part of the closet. Another short double window was on the back wall and, as in Bonnie's room, there was just barely enough room to walk around the bed.

"C'mon, Mom, now you gotta see our bathroom," she said and threw open the closed door.

It was a sunken bathroom. We had to step down about eight inches onto a tiled floor, and we were in a room that was as large as Bonnie's bedroom. Immediately to the left was a western-styled toilet stool with a wooden water closet high on the wall above it with a hanging chain for flushing. A small lavatory was on the far end of the right wall, and an ordinary old-fashioned bathtub with legs sat almost in the middle of the room under faucets extending about twelve to fifteen inches out of the wall. Bill told me there was just a hole in the floor under the tub for drainage, and added, "We can move the tub around any way you want it."

"Now you gotta see the kitchen, Mom." Coming out of the bathroom, I got just a glimpse of the back of a black-haired girl entering the kitchen. Bill had written that he'd hired a maid, but in all our excitement I'd completely forgotten about her.

"Kimiko, come here. I want you to meet my wife and daughter."

A slightly stocky Japanese girl approached us with short, cautious steps, the straw slippers on her bare feet slapping on the floor. As she stood before me, shorter than I, with her head slightly lowered and her eyes looking at the floor in an attitude of servitude, I felt uncomfortable wondering how I should speak to her. I wasn't accustomed to having servants, let alone a foreign one.

Slipping his arm around my shoulders, Bill said, "Kimiko, this is my wife, Geil, and the little one here," patting Bonnie on the top of her head, "is my daughter, Bonnie."

Kimiko bowed low saying something softly in Japanese. Then standing erect, looking at me with her clear, deep brown eyes shaped like little upside down half-moons, said, "Halo," and then with a big smile dimpling her round, full cheeks, said, "Hi, Bonnie-chan."

Bill apparently felt the tenseness in my body during the introductions, and took command. "Kimiko, why don't you help Bonnie put her things away. We've got to get that pile of luggage out of the middle of the room. "

Bonnie dived into the pile and started digging and pulling out her things, chatting away, with Kimiko helping her.

I went on into the kitchen, not only to see what it was like but to try to regain control of myself, or maybe I was subconsciously avoiding Kimiko as long as possible.

The kitchen was smaller than the bathroom. Immediately inside the door on the left was a GI refrigerator. A small window was next to it under which was a rusty tin sink sitting in an unfinished wooden frame with small work areas at both ends. As in the bathroom, the water faucets came out of the wall. At the end of the sink and work area the wooden ledge continued on around to the right for about a yard upon which sat a small, two-burner gas stove, very much like the little rustic ones furnished in fishing cabins back in the States. Standing against the right wall was a narrow cupboard, approximately four feet long and about fifty inches high, with wooden sliding doors. The width between the sink and cupboard was just wide enough for one person. And back in a little alcove was the hot water heater.

"Hey, Mom, I'm hungry," Bonnie said. "Can I have something to eat?"

Good heavens, I thought, it was past two o'clock and none of us had had anything to eat since very early that morning.

"Say, I'm hungry, too," Bill agreed. "I got a few groceries in, Geil. Not many, but see if you can't find something to fix for us, and we'll go to the commissary later on and stock up."

I started rummaging around in the kitchen, found bacon and eggs in the refrigerator, and located some bread, coffee and canned fruit. "How about bacon and egg sandwiches?"

"Sounds fine. Just anything."

"Where's the skillet?"

"I don't know. It's out there someplace. I got dishes, silverware, pots and pans—the whole works—from Supply, so there should be anything you need."

It just wasn't my kitchen, and I didn't know where to start. I went in and whispered to Bill, "Would it be okay if we have Kimiko do the cooking? I don't know where anything is, and I'm not even sure how to work that stove."

"Sure, she can do it. She's done a little cooking for me the last few days." He asked Kimiko to fix our lunch, told her how we each liked our eggs, and in a reasonably short time she had fixed our lunch.

Ready to sit down, I noticed she'd set the table for three. What about Kimiko? I knew she must be hungry, too. But where was she to eat? Should she eat in the kitchen? Had she brought her own Japanese food? Somehow I just couldn't discuss this with Bill in front of Kimiko, as I felt it would be as embarrassing to her as it would be to me. I wasn't sure whether it was proper or acceptable for a Japanese maid to sit at the same table with her employers, and I wasn't quite sure that I approved of that either. But a quick decision had to be made. It seemed rude to make her stay in the kitchen alone and eat standing up. So, right or wrong, I invited her to join us at the table if she wished.

Kimiko served our meal with a quiet compliancy, then unobtrusively joined us at the table and we all heartily partook of the simple fare as though dining sumptuously.

Our tummies full, most of our clothing put away, and Kimiko busy in the kitchen cleaning up, we were at a loss what to do. Our attempt at conversation resulted in trivial chit-chat and we were forcing even that. We were suddenly like strangers. Mental and physical tiredness were overtaking all three of us, so Bill dismissed Kimiko when she'd finished the dishes and we retired for a much needed nap.

Awakening from that restful sleep, we were surprised to see that the cloudiness of the gray day had given way to dusk and, turning on the radio to check the time, discovered it was too late to go to the commissary. None of us particularly wanted to eat eggs again, so we would have to go to a restaurant. Bill told us the First Three Graders Club in downtown Tokyo had good food, but since we'd have to go by bus it would take several hours to ride down, eat, and then the return ride, even if he knew the bus schedules, which he didn't.

"Isn't there someplace nearer where we can eat?" I asked. "I'm too tired to do anymore traveling today unless I just have to."

"There's a small PX restaurant over on Grant Heights," he replied, "but I don't know what kind of food it's got."

"Well, let's go there. It surely can't be too bad."

The day had been moderately warm, but Bill warned us the night winter air in Tokyo was very cold and damp and we should dress warmly. Bundled up in our heavy winter coats, we descended to street level and hopefully waited for a bus. Bonnie, seeing the stores down the street, wanted to look at them. We started walking along the street towards Grant Heights. Bill was watching over his shoulder for a bus, Bonnie was lured on by the little open shops, and I, wary of Bonnie slipping in a store while I was trying to keep Bill in my sights, was trying not to lose either of them.

At the entrance to Grant Heights (a housing area for military and civilian employees and their dependents) we stood around for a while thinking surely a bus would come along, but none were forthcoming. The sky was darkening by the minute, the cold was biting at our extremities, and it was necessary to keep moving to keep our blood circulating. Rather than just pacing in circles, flapping our arms, we headed in the general direction of the PX. Instead of following the street, Bill decided on a short-cut across the sod. We'd only traveled a short distance when night's black shroud dropped over everything, even eliminating the stars and lighted windows. Not being able to see where we were walking and to help break the cutting wind, I wrapped my scarf around my head, turned up my big coat collar, and entwined my arms around Bill's arm. Bonnie pressed close to his other side, hanging on to his hand. And the three of us, as though welded together, stumbled through the pitch black night in search of the PX.

We were chilled to the bones by the time we reached it and lingered over the food, sipping lots of hot coffee until the warmth of the food and restaurant thawed our bodies, fortifying us for the long, cold, dark trek back to our house.

The little warmth the kerosene heater was emitting felt good, but it didn't seem to be circulating into the bedrooms. Digging out our flannel pajamas and donning some of Bill's woolen socks, we piled about four woolen Army blankets and comforters on our beds in the hope of getting warm again. Snuggled down under the covers, not even waiting for my body temperature to rise to normal, I slipped off into a sound, deep sleep; and thus brought to an end my first day in Japan—Thursday, December 9, 1954.

9

Bill had given Kimiko the rest of that week off until the following Monday as he was on leave and able to be with us. For the first time in a long time none of us had to be up early to be at work, school or to answer for some other duty, so we luxuriously remained in bed thereby catching up on our rest and also giving the warmth of the day an opportunity to replace the cold of the night. Bonnie and her dad were completely rejuvenated. I felt rested, although my body ached with stiffness due to the cold night and from the heavy weight of the bedding.

Gingerly I faced the problem of preparing some brunch, but welcomed the opportunity of being left on my own to explore the kitchen and all its contents. Bonnie rapidly fired questions at her father, hardly waiting for answers, in typical childlike curiosity to learn, see and do all things at once.

In the confines of our little house, with no strangers or intruders and free of all inhibitions, we became our normal selves exchanging with each other various experiences and anecdotes of the past several months of separation. Eventually, our discourse brought us up to the present and the various tasks and plans that needed to be taken care of, especially those that Bill would have to help us with before he returned to duty.

Bonnie had missed a good month of school, and it was important to get her enrolled and back in routine as soon as possible. The school for American dependents was situated on Grant Heights. Bill grumbled about not having our car yet to drive us to the diversely scattered places we had to go; however, a military bus stopped for us and we were on our way to the school.

The school was a large, two-story, frame building in which we located the office, presented Bonnie's report card and immunization record, got her registered and assigned to the fifth grade. Directed to the second floor, we met her teacher, who advised us that she was giving examinations that day and Bonnie might as well wait until the following Monday to start school. Proceeding on to the commissary, we stocked up on groceries and rode the bus home. Our first items of business having been taken care of in a relatively short time prompted us to walk back to Grant Heights for a bus to downtown Tokyo.

Our house was in the outskirts of Tokyo, so it was a rather lengthy ride downtown and was my first good chance to see Japan. What a myriad of sights. Most of the houses were unpainted, weathered frame buildings with sliding doors and windows, some with tile roofs, and built right next to each other. A great number of the houses facing the street had small shops set up in the front part of the dwelling. What should have been sidewalks were in the majority either plain, hard-packed dirt, cobblestones or gravel, and in rare instances small squares of cement laid in narrow paths. Only about fifty percent, or less, of the people we saw were in native attire, the rest being in Western-style clothes.

The traffic situation alone was an interesting sight. Big busses, big trucks, trolley cars, ordinary sized left-hand drive automobiles, midget-sized right-hand drive English and Japanese made autos, three-wheeled trucks (nothing more than motorcycles with a built-on cab and rack), motorcycles, millions of bicycles with some pulling two-wheeled carts and others with a package or some item tied on it somewhere, hand-drawn carts, pushcarts, variable wagons and carts pulled by bulls or oxen, and many, many, many people literally milling all over the streets, sidewalks and any other place available. As we neared the downtown area, buildings were large as in any city, and the streets were wider, permitting more vehicles to race around and more people to mill around causing more congestion.

We had to transfer twice before we reached our destination, Hardy Barracks. It was the Headquarters of the American Eighth Army and the Military Advisory and Assistance

Group to Japan. A white cement, eight-story, octagon-shaped building, it had previously been a dormitory for the best troops of the Japanese Army during World War II. Bill worked here so we visited his office, met the people with whom he worked, then proceeded with getting our ration books, identification cards, overseas driver's license, etc.

Our long ride downtown, plus all the forms we had to fill out, used up more time than we had anticipated and consequently we didn't get finished before the offices closed, and we had to return home. The night's darkness again brought the bitter cold with it forcing us to retire early in the hope of staying warm, but to no avail.

10

With only two days left before Bonnie would start school and Kimiko's return as a full-time maid, I was intent on getting our daily routine organized into familiar stateside living, mindful, however, of making a few concessions.

The day started off as an ordinary Saturday. I busied myself with tidying up the house, Bonnie cleaned her room, although she did a lot of complaining as she wanted to leave it for Kimiko to do. Bill was checking the appliances and haphazardly showing me how to operate the stove, hot water and kerosene heaters, explaining that Pappa-san, employed by our landlord as a handyman for all five houses, would take care of refilling the fuel and do other little odd jobs I needed to have done from time to time.

The house seemed to be taking a long time to warm up and intermittently Bill or I would turn up the heat control. But regardless of the setting, that stove radiated only a minimum of heat. While Bill was tinkering with it, I glanced through a US Government booklet about living and staying healthy in Japan. Reading with a negative mind, all I absorbed was information about the hidden dangers of dining in Japanese restaurants, eating locally produced fruit, vegetables, meat, poultry and fish, and about the drinking water.

"Hey, Bill," I said, "what about the water in this house?"

"What about it?"

"I mean, is it OK to drink?"

"No, maybe better not. You'd better boil it first. There's some in the refrigerator if you want a drink."

Oh, my God, I thought, did Bonnie or I drink any from the faucet out of habit? I sure hoped we hadn't and hurriedly got the biggest pan I could find, boiled some water and cautioned Bonnie to drink only the boiled water.

"I'm going over to the PX," Bill said disgustedly, "and get an electric heater. I can't find what's wrong, but this damn stove's not working right and I'll be damned if we're going to sit around and freeze again tonight."

He slammed the door as he walked out.

Having been married to him for fifteen years, I knew the minute he started swearing he was upset and it was absolutely useless of me to mention I'd like to go with him because I was afraid to stay alone. Locking the door and trying to hide my feelings from Bonnie, I half-heartedly engaged her in some games, but kept one ear attuned for the sound of a bus and Bill's return. Following a couple of disappointments, we saw him get off a bus with a big package and ran down to meet him. Climbing back up the stairs we met an Air Force officer coming down.

"Major, I'd like you to meet my . . . "

"Hey, I know you," he said pointing at me. "I didn't know she was your wife, Sergeant." The major flashed a friendly grin towards me, "You used to work in Headquarters at Scott, didn't you?"

"Y—yes," I stuttered.

"Sure, I know. You worked in A-4, didn't you?"

"Why yes, that's right," I said and wrinkled my brow trying to remember his name. It'd been five or six years since we had been stationed at Scott Air Force Base near Belleville, Illinois.

"Glad to have you as our new neighbor, Mrs. Butler. We'll all have to get together for a drink," he said and hurried on down the steps.

"That was Major Ley," Bill said, finishing his introduction. "They live next door to us. I knew him when I worked on the flight line at Scott and he was doing a lot of flying."

Our new electric heater was hooked up and was a most welcome addition. As the heat was diffused, our bodies absorbed the warmth as a sponge soaks up water. Bill relaxed in a chair, listening to the radio, and fought a losing battle to keep his eyelids open. I was writing a letter and Bonnie was restlessly going through her few toys and books looking for something to do.

"What'd you turn the radio down for?" Bill asked me and he turned the volume up, "I'm listening to it."

"I didn't touch the radio," I replied. "Even if I did, how would you know? You've been asleep."

"I have not. Just because my eyes are closed doesn't mean I'm asleep." The sound of the radio dimmed. "Now, what the hell's wrong?"

He again turned up the volume, and again the sound faded. He turned the knob as far as it would go, but the sound continued to fade until we could barely hear it. "Well, that does that. I might as well go try to find a booster now or forget about having a radio."

"Where're you going, Daddy? Can I go too?" Bonnie wasn't taking any chances of being left behind this time.

"Just down the street to get something for the radio. You and Mommie might as well come with me. I don't know how long it'll take me or how far I'll have to go to find one."

The little shops edging the street were wide open with no front walls. Just walking past them we could see what they had for sale and each shop seemed to specialize in its own unique merchandise: bamboo, fruit, fish, china, silver, etc. We zigzagged through a few Bill thought might have what he was looking for, giving Bonnie and me a chance for a closer look at things, but he kept pushing on intent upon finding a booster.

One exceptionally small shop we nearly bypassed had some electric bulbs, plugs and cords. We walked into the cramped, over-crowded store and Bill began a methodical search through the wares. A kimono-clad Japanese woman emerged from a back room, bowed to us, speaking in her native tongue. We acknowledged her greeting with a slight nod. Bill told her what we needed. She just stood there looking at him.

"Just my luck, she doesn't understand English," Bill said, thinking out loud, so he continued his search.

I had no idea what a booster was or what it looked like, so I just stood and waited.

"Here's one that might do," Bill said, picking up a small box-like affair.

When the Japanese woman saw what Bill had, she bowed and disappeared into the back room, returning with her arms filled with several different models and styles of little boxes. She sat them all on a small counter and she and Bill began talking, each in their own language, and twisting the dials and in general checking each make thoroughly. As Bill had had two previous tours of duty in the Far East, he understood some Japanese and was able to determine from their conversation and the actions of the saleslady, added to his own knowledge, which model was best. She wrote the price down in Arabic figures and he paid her in yen, the Japanese currency.

I was intrigued by how carefully and neatly she wrapped our purchase, tying it with paper string in such a way as to leave a little loop at one end to hook a finger through with which to carry it. As we left the store she was bowing again and saying something in Japanese, which Bill interpreted as being, "Thank you very much."

Back home the irritations of trying to fix supper started erratic thoughts: This stupid, dinky kitchen. There's no place to work. What do I do now? I need three burners to cook the steak, potatoes and a vegetable, and there's only two. And not even an oven—and that dirty, smelly heater. How I hate that. I wish I could get warm, really warm, just once—and no telephone. But I don't know anyone anyway. So many things I need, how will I ever get them? I don't know where to look for them, I don't know the language, I don't understand their money—Heavens, there are so many things to worry about. I'll just never leave the house, that's what. I'd get lost for sure. I've been lost in a hotel when I've turned two corners. In fact, I was even lost on the boat. You'd think my own husband would be so glad to see me he'd be out here helping me. ...

The struggle of getting the food all prepared combined with my ever-increasing tension, affected not only my appetite (the food felt like rocks in my stomach), but affected my whole attitude and I didn't bother trying to conceal my dejection. Bill and Bonnie were unusually quiet as they ate, but all I could think about was me—how horrible I felt, how scared I was, how rough it was on me, and oh, how I wished I were back home in the States.

When we'd finished eating, I couldn't bring myself to go back in that horrible kitchen right away and fight the unhandiness of getting things cleaned up and put away. As I sat there trying to calm down, the flimsy construction of the house was emphasized as the strange, eerie noises floated in from the street and sounded as if they were right outside the door. Terror welled up inside me, adding to my already overwrought emotions.

"Wotz-zat?" I hissed at Bill, my body stiffening.

"Somebody knocking at the door. What's the matter with you?" he snarled at me as he went to the door. Bonnie scooted over and crowded in the chair with me.

"Well, I'll be darned. Hi! Come on in. What are you doing here?"

"That's a fine greeting. What are we doing here? We came to welcome your wife to Japan," I heard a woman's voice say, and in walked Faye and Van, old friends from another duty station. "Welcome to Japan, Geil. How are you? Bill told us when you were to arrive and we had to come see you," Faye continued. "Hi, Bonnie, how are you?"

"Why, hello," I said and jumped up, almost knocking Bonnie out of the chair. "This is quite a surprise. I wasn't expecting any company. Here, sit down," and I offered them the only two comfortable chairs in the room.

"Hi, Bonnie. Hi, Geil, nice to see you again," Van said and clasped my hand warmly.

"Here, let me take your coats," Bill said and took them and pulled out the wooden chairs for us.

"If we've interrupted your dinner, Geil, please go ahead. Don't mind us."

"No. No, we've just finished." My face flushed as I hastily stacked the dirty dishes and carried them to the kitchen.

"What's new, Van?" Bill asked. "You got that hospital and those doctors whipped into shape yet?" And with that, he drew the attention away from me and got them into a discussion of service life. Van had been commissioned as an administrative officer in the Medical Corps since we'd been neighbors at Scott and they were now stationed at Johnson Air Force Base, about thirty minutes from Tokyo.

Without any warning, our lights started flickering, getting dimmer and finally went out. There we sat in total darkness other than the glimmer of flashing lights as cars and busses passed on the street below.

"You must have blown a fuse," Van offered.

"Maybe," Bill answered, "but first I think I'll check the other houses and see if they have lights." He and Van went outside.

"Well, how do you like Japan, Geil?"

Boy, was that ever a loaded question coming right then. All during their glib prattling, instead of rejoicing at seeing old friends, I continued wallowing in self-pity, thinking: There sits Faye with her make-up artfully applied, every hair in her head in place, and all dressed up fancy as the Queen of Sheba; and here I am—hair a mess, no make-up, wearing bright green, wrinkled slacks, Bill's olive drab woolen sweater, his black wool socks, and my fluorescent pink fuzzy bedroom slippers, looking like I'd just come from Lower Slobovia.

"I hate it!" I answered vehemently. "I wish I could go home tomorrow."

"Oh, everyone feels like that when they first arrive. But you'll like it when you've been here awhile and get quarters. You're going to have a maid, aren't you?"

"Yes, we've got one."

"Well, see, you won't have anything to do. You won't be tied down with Bonnie. You can go shopping. Everything's so cheap, you know. And parties—your maid will stay at night, won't she? I mean, you don't have to worry about getting a baby sitter for Bonnie, and ..."

She continued chortling in her Texan drawl about Japan until I thought I'd lose my senses. She was my friend and was just trying to be nice to me, but—

"I don't care," I said thinking out loud, not really answering her. "I hate this place; I'll never like it. I just wish I'd never come!"

Apparently my words were like a slap in the face to her. She didn't say another word. Thank goodness, Bill and Van returned then—or had they heard me, too?

"None of the houses have any lights," Bill reported. "Some woman told me it was my fault 'cause she saw me bringing in the heater today. Well, I don't give a damn what she thinks. The major said the transformer isn't big enough for all these houses and they turn it off sometimes to let it cool down.

"Do you know where the candles are, Geil?"

"No. I haven't seen any."

"Well, damn it, there's some around here someplace," he said, and using his cigarette lighter, he started looking around in the kitchen.

"Don't bother, Bill," Faye called to him as she stood up. "We really should be going. Where'd you put our coats?"

"They're in Bonnie's room. But you don't have to rush off," Bill said as he returned with his lighter and led the way to the bedroom.

"Say, since you don't have your car yet and you have all that running around to do downtown getting the rest of Geil's papers, why don't you let Faye come in Monday and drive you around?" Van volunteered.

"Ah, that's too much bother."

"No, no bother," Faye told him. I don't mind at all. I don't have any plans for Monday and I'd be glad to do it."

"Well, if you're sure you don't mind, it'd sure be a big help," Bill replied.

I knew how he hated to have to depend on someone else, but I also knew how impatient he got at having to depend on the uncertainty of the bus travel. How kind it was of them to offer, but I couldn't say the words out loud.

"OK, fine. I'll see you-all Monday morning. Nice seeing you again, Geil. G'night," Faye said and led the way out and they were gone.

Bonnie had clutched my hand and hung on for dear life ever since the lights had gone out and we three just sat there, not saying a word. What had happened to me? I couldn't remember ever having been so rude to anyone as I'd just been to Faye and Van. I was sure they'd cut their visit short because I was such a poor hostess. Why, I hadn't even offered them a cup of coffee. But, I probably couldn't have made any anyhow.

When the lights finally came back on, I helped Bonnie get ready for bed, tucked her in, and then went to bed myself. "Oh, dear Lord," I prayed, "help me. I'm so homesick, unhappy, and scared."

I could hear Bill banging around getting ready to retire and instinctively knew he was putting off coming to bed so he wouldn't have to talk to me. And I was sure now he'd overheard me tell Faye I wish I'd never come to Japan. Not wanting to have a show-down with him, I feigned sleep, buried my head in the pillow to stifle my sobs, and cried myself to sleep.

11

The kerosene heater had gone off during the night and the house was like an ice box when we woke up the next morning. I passed off my low spirits and my obvious swollen, red eyes and runny nose due to coming down with a cold. Bonnie got a blanket and wrapped herself up in it and curled up in a chair next to the electric heater. I did the same thing, pretending to write a letter. Bill left the house, not bothering to tell me where he was going or what he was going to do, but I didn't care. I didn't care about anything anymore. I knew I was trapped, like in quicksand, sinking ever so slowly and, numbed with fear, I just wanted to be put out of my misery.

Bill returned with a Japanese man whom he introduced to us as Pappa-san and informed us he was the handy man that worked there.

"He's going to help me tear this heater down and see if we can't get it fixed."

Pappa-san, standing just inside the door, acknowledged us by a slight nod of the head, removed his shoes (nothing more than woven straw soles held on his bare feet by black velveteen straps), and slipped off his fleece-lined jacket (looking like it might have come from any Army surplus store), laying it on the floor by his shoes. Bill and Pappa-san went right to work on the stove and I, not saying a word, just watched them in their labors.

After checking, poking, turning dials and going over everything, they carefully removed one piece after another, meticulously laying them out in an orderly fashion, every now and then trying unsuccessfully to get the stove started. Pappa-san only spoke a few words of broken English, but he and Bill managed a communication of sorts and worked very well together—Bill knowing basically what had to be done, and Pappa-san's experienced nimble fingers helping out at just the right moment.

They were so intent on their work that I could really look at Pappa-san and not worry about being caught staring. His patched, clean white shirt and faded khaki trousers, belted with a piece of rope, loosely hung on his small, wiry body. He appeared approximately four and a half feet tall, but looked shorter in his over-sized clothing standing beside my 5'8" husband. As he worked he squatted, balancing on stubby, calloused feet, his toes widespread from years of wearing thongs; and with each uncertainty or new difficulty he would spread his lips, suck air in through his teeth making a "hissing" sound and sort of shake his head to one side in bewilderment. He wore a black baseball cap, showing just a bit of short-cropped gray hair; and tucked in beneath his dark eyebrows were brown, slanted eyes. His cheeks were firm, and I couldn't tell whether the few wrinkles were from age or weathered from working outdoors. I judged his age to be somewhere between forty and fifty.

"Ah, ha! I think this just might be what's causing all the trouble," Bill said as he held up a sooty, little thing-a-ma-jig in his greasy hand.

"Ah, so," Pappa-san hissed and nodded his head in agreement. He left the house and returned shortly with some tools and pieces of metal.

He and Bill worked arduously with those dirty little pieces. They tediously reassembled the heater, cleaning each dirty piece before returning it to its proper place, until there were no pieces remaining. Bill lit the stove, the flame blazed up, and then settled down operating normally, and it was soon sending out good, warm heat.

12

Out of the habit of going to school, Bonnie was torn between the excitement and anticipation of being with children her own age and the consternation and fear of going to a new school, making new friends and riding a bus. To make it easier, I decided to ride with her that first morning. Trying to assume a confidence I didn't have, we hopefully waited for the bus while every passing Japanese stared at us as long as they could. What a relief when a bus stopped and picked us up.

I walked with Bonnie to her room. The teacher explained there was a regular GI school bus for the children and she would see that Bonnie got on the right bus after school. Bonnie looked imploringly at me, and the terror in her eyes tugged at my heartstrings as much as her little hand clung to mine, not wanting me to leave. Reassuring her I would meet her after school and ride home with her, I hurriedly departed so she wouldn't see the tears in my eyes.

Kimiko had arrived and Bill was telling her we had to go downtown and what time Bonnie would be out of school in case we didn't get back in time. He hadn't approved of my riding to school with Bonnie that morning, and not wanting to pour fuel on our already strained relations, I refrained from telling him I had promised Bonnie I would meet her. We'd just have to cross that bridge when we came to it.

Riding in a car seemed more hazardous than riding a bus. Faye drove, with Bill in the front watching out for traffic and directing her to the different places. We had to get ration books (chocolate, cocoa, shoes, cigarettes, permanent waves, etc., were rationed in the PX); identification cards (not only our American ID cards, but also Japanese as MAAG-J was a part of the American Embassy rather than strictly military); driver's licenses (American and Japanese); and finally to the Daiichi Hotel to register for the overall evacuation plan (listing our names and address, age, sex, stateside permanent address, next of kin, etc., in case of any emergency). At the hotel we saw two Russian Army officers, impressing on me the importance of this latter detail and added more to my anxieties.

With all the red-tape of filling out endless forms, I'd lost track of time until Faye suggested we stop at the First Three Graders Club for a late lunch. The food was good and the stateside atmosphere of the club was a welcome change, but the hour was growing late and I was in a hurry to get home and gulped down my food, hoping that Faye and Bill would do the same. But, they seemed to be enjoying the food and each other's company.

When we finally headed towards home I thought there was a chance we might make it in time until Faye drove in the parking lot at the Finance Building to go to the large Tokyo PX. She said she hadn't been there for some time and wanted to see what new things had arrived. She told me she thought I'd enjoy it, too, as it had so much more to choose from than at Grant Heights. She had been considerate in driving us around to take care of our business and Bill seemed interested in stopping at the PX, so I never said a word and just tagged along not really looking at anything.

It was after four o'clock when we finally got back to our house and I was really worried about Bonnie. With only a quick "thanks" to Faye, I dashed up the steps, threw open the door, and was relieved to see that Bonnie was home. Then I saw she'd been crying.

"Mommie, Mommie," she said as she ran to me, throwing her arms around me and squeezing my neck so tight I could hardly breathe. "You said you'd meet me and you weren't there! And I was so scared I'd get on the wrong bus." The tears started flowing down her cheeks anew.

"Honey, there, there," I said, hugging her as I wiped away her tears. "I'm so sorry, but it just couldn't be helped."

"You dai-jobu now, Bonnie-chan," Kimiko said, patting Bonnie on the shoulder. "Your Mamma-san's home now, you dai-jobu."

Bonnie managed a tearful smile for Kimiko, and then told

me, "Mommie, it was awful. I didn't know when to pull the string, and when I did pull it he stopped way up the street. I was so scared. Then I saw Kimiko, and she walked home with me, and then I didn't know where you were ... and, Kimiko's been playing games with me waiting for you to come home."

God bless Kimiko, I thought. How can I ever thank her enough?

"Bonnie-chan so worried about you," Kimiko told me, "but she dai-jobu now, you home now."

"Thank you, Kimiko," I said, inadequately trying to relay my deep gratitude. "That was very nice what you did."

Thinking I could get Bonnie's mind off of the upsetting experience of the bus ride home only to find us gone, I asked her about her first day of school.

"Oh, Mommie," she said and I thought she was going to start crying again. "It was awful. I hate it. I don't ever want to go back. I don't know anybody..."

"Well, honey, you'll get acquainted. If you're friendly to them, they'll be friendly to you."

"No, they won't. I tried. And I don't even have a desk—I had to bring all my books home."

"Surely you didn't stand up all day, did you?"

"No."

"Well, where did you sit?"

"They found an old chair and I had to sit way in the back at a big old table."

"Couldn't you have left your books on the table, and just brought home the ones you needed for your homework?"

"Oh, Mommie, you don't understand. It was just a big old table with lots of books and papers and stuff on it and I was afraid someone would take my books, or they'd get lost or something."

"Okay, I'm sorry. I understand...," I said, deciding I wasn't helping matters. Anyway you looked at it, it had been an exceptionally rough first day of school on a little nine-year-old, and then the disappointment of her mother's broken promise, and lastly the abandoned feeling when she found her parents not at home. Boy, what a mess. Just one more reason for wishing I'd never come to Japan.

"Hi, Mrs. Ley," I heard Bill say.

I'd forgotten all about Faye and Bill in my concern for Bonnie. Apparently Faye had left, as I didn't see her.

"Come on in. Geil, this is Mrs. Ley, our next door neighbor. Mrs. Ley, this is my wife, Geil, and daughter, Bonnie."

"Hi, Geil and Bonnie, nice to meet you." The woman, an attractive, petite blonde, dressed in navy blue slacks and sweater, came in the house and said,"This is the first chance I've had to get over since Ed saw you and said he knew you. Small world, isn't it?" A small, blonde-headed girl and two active little boys came running in behind her. "Sorry about these," she said, pointing to her children. "That's Nancy, Roddy and Jeff. I tried to get away without them, but they followed me anyhow."

"Hi, nice to meet you," I answered, and there was something so warm and friendly in her eyes and manner that I really was glad to meet her. The children were friends immediately, and Bonnie took them in her room and shared her toys with them.

"We just got back a few minutes ago from downtown Tokyo—"

"Yes, I know. It's a mess, isn't it, getting all that stuff done."

She was the first person I'd talked to that seemed to understand how I felt and sympathized with me, so I told her of Bonnie's rough day. She apologized for not coming over sooner to help, told me Bonnie could ride to school with Jeff and the other children living there, and ended up by asking me over for coffee the following morning.

"C'mon, kids, we're going now," she called, "and I'll see you for coffee tomorrow, Geil."

"Ah, do we have to go?" all the children said at once.

"Yes, right now. After all, Bonnie is going to be living right next door to you, and you can see her every day."

With that they were all gone. Their brief visit had been like a breath of fresh air in a smoke-filled room. Bonnie had forgotten her troubles and I'd gotten the definite impression that here was someone I could talk to that felt about Japan as I did, or at least understood how I felt.

"She seems real nice," I told Bill.

"She's quite a gal," Bill answered. "I sure hope you two can hit it off. She's been here about six months and can be a big help to you—I hate to tell you this, but I have to go back to work tomorrow."

"Oh, no. How come?" I could feel myself sinking again.

"They told me today when we were at the office. Something's come up I have to do. I'm sorry, but you know how it is."

Yes, I knew how it was. I'd been connected with the military long enough to know that orders can suddenly be changed. I even courted the idea that perhaps Bill had volunteered to return to duty to get away from me. And I also knew about protocol and, even though Mrs. Ley had been so generous in offering her assistance, a sergeant's wife just doesn't ask a major's wife for help. And besides, I was no better off with our other neighbors. Two of the families were officers (an Army captain and an Air Force major) and the other civilians, a man and wife who both worked. I was in a pretty kettle of fish. My bitter ranting on all of this was the last straw for Bill.

"Sure, I know who our neighbors are. But you ought to be damn glad you've got this kind of house to live in so near a housing area. Most sergeants can't afford a place this good, and we couldn't either if I wasn't with the MAAG-J. They're picking up the tab for the extra this place costs over my quarters allowance. You should just see some of the places other people have to live in. If you had to live there, you'd really have something to bitch about. You ought to know me well enough by now to know that I wouldn't let you and Bonnie live in a hovel stuck out someplace away from other Americans. I can't understand you. I don't know what's wrong with you. You've never been like this. If you keep this up, the way you've been, by God you can just go home. It's no joy for me having you here if you're going to be like this."

His yelling and swearing brought tears welling up in my eyes, a big lump filled my throat, and I tried to shut his words out by withdrawing into myself and feeling sorry for myself again. But the more he talked I knew he was right and that I had every bit of it coming.

"I got hot water, Serlgeant. I fix you bath now, dai-jobu?"

"No thanks, Kimiko. Not now. You can go home now."

When she'd left, I turned to Bill. "What was that all about? Was she going to give you a bath? I've heard they do that. She sure waits on you hand and foot."

"Look, she didn't mean a thing. Not what you're thinking, anyway. She was only doing her job. Japanese women are trained from the time they're little girls to wait on men, do things for them, make them comfortable. So, don't go getting any ideas, and don't cause trouble with her. She's a good maid, and I interviewed about forty before I found her."

None of us ate much supper. I took Bonnie in her bedroom and helped her with her homework, and Bill went to bed shortly afterwards.

13

Bill left for work around dawn, saying very little to me that morning. Bonnie didn't want to go to school, but half-heartedly joined Jeff and the other children to wait for the bus after I again promised to meet her and ride home with her. With both of them gone, I could feel an awful loneliness engulfing me. This would be my first day all alone with Kimiko, and I wasn't sure yet how to treat her or how to act around her.

"Hey, Geil," I heard a voice call, "aren't you coming over for coffee?"

Oh, my gosh, I'd forgotten all about Mrs. Ley's invitation. "I didn't know if you really meant it."

"Of course, I meant it. C'mon in, it's all ready."

The coffee and rich French pastries were delicious, and I particularly enjoyed Mrs. Ley's friendly, relaxed manner. We were soon chatting about the hardships of our separate ocean voyages and usual woman talk.

"Please stop calling me Mrs. Ley," she told me. "My name's Jeanne. Look, I know what a rough time it is riding a bus with sacks of groceries. I've been through it. Ed's in a car pool and I get the car two or three times a week and I'd be happy to give you a lift whenever I go. We've only got an old Ford station wagon, but it sure beats walking or riding the bus."

"Thanks so much. I appreciate that."

The arrival of our hold baggage interrupted our coffee, but at least it gave me something to do. Kimiko was excited about the "new" things, and our mutual preoccupation of unpacking and putting things away knocked down a few of the barriers between us as I tried to explain to her what some of the things were and how they worked. When we'd finished, Kimiko went on about her work, making me feel like a stranger in my own home and, at a loss what to do, I went to bed. I don't know of anything more tiring than boredom and idleness.

"Oku-san. Oku-san." Subconsciously I was aware of a strange voice.

"Oku-san, dozo." Someone seemed to be shaking my shoulder. "More better you get up now and go get Bonnie-chan."

I was in such a deep, sound sleep I couldn't remember where I was or who was talking.

"Huh, what'd you say?" I asked, trying to force my eyes open.

"More better you get up now and go get Bonnie-chan."

"Oh, golly, what time is it?" I asked groggily. "Is it that late? I must have really zonked out."

Splashing cold water on my face to get rid of my grogginess, I grabbed my coat and put it on as I was dashing out to catch the bus. Thanks to Kimiko, I made it in time.

When Bonnie and I returned home, the gloomy, dreary clouds that had curtained the skies since our arrival in Japan parted and let the sun shine through which lifted our spirits immeasurably.

"Look, Oku-san, Bonnie-chan." Kimiko was pointing out our front windows. "You see Fuji-ama?" Sure enough, we could see beautiful Mount Fuji towering majestically over the city, its snow covered peak sparkling in the sunlight.

Bill arrived home about 6 p.m., welcomed by the aroma of food cooking, the little homey additions and changes in the house, and a less tense wife and daughter.

During our "lights-out" session he explained the strange clippity-clop, clippity-clop sounds outside were made by the wooden getas (shoes) of the people walking along the street below. The eerie wailing was the reedy flute-like music announcing the arrival of hot food being sold from a little push-cart. And he explained he'd interviewed so many maids before hiring Kimiko because he wanted one that had worked for Americans, who understood and spoke fairly good English. He chose Kimiko because he thought she would be the most help to me, not necessarily around the house doing the work, but more importantly as an interpreter and go-between since we lived in private rental. Consequently, we agreed Kimiko should work from 8 a.m. to 5:30 p.m., so I wouldn't have to be alone when Bonnie and Bill were gone, but neither would I have to share my family during the short morning and evening hours. Anyhow, I preferred to do my own cooking.

Bill was pleased that we were able to communicate and that I was at least acting more like a human being.

14

Disliking idleness and not wanting to sleep another day of my life away, I tackled the chore of addressing Christmas cards. The task of writing to and thinking about all our friends and relatives back home soon became too depressing.

It was inevitable in our small house that Kimiko and I started talking, haltingly at first, with her repeating words until I understood her accent.

Bill had warned me that all Japanese have a way of saying "Hai" or "Yes" to everything you say, whether they understand or not, so I decided right now was a good time to get this settled between Kimiko and me.

"Kimiko, if I talk too fast, or if you don't understand me, you will ask me what I mean, won't you?"

"Hai, I know."

The bare windows in the bedrooms were really bothering me and, tired of writing letters, I asked, "Kimiko, do you know where I can buy some curtain rods?"

"Curltain lods? I no understand."

"You know, something to hang the curtains on over the windows? Is there a dime store, or hardware store near by?"

Sucking air in through her teeth, she cocked her head at me, "Wot's a wot-you-say store?"

"A place where they sell screws, metal rods—something to put up here so we can hang up the curtains," I said and demonstrated at the window with my hands.

"Hai, I sink so."

"Would you mind going with me?"

"Hai."

Oh dear, didn't she want to go with me? I didn't think I could do it alone. I suppose I could send her out to get them, but from the bewildered expression on her face, I wasn't sure she understood what I wanted. If I could just get her to go with me, I could look until I found something, and she could be my interpreter and do the buying for me—But wait a minute, I thought. I think I asked that question wrong.

"Would you go with me, Kimiko?" I asked.

"Hai, I go."

"Good. How far do you think we'll have to go?

"Oh, maybe five minutes."

I'd expected an answer of so many blocks, but five minutes didn't sound too bad. Kimiko was used to walking and set a pretty fast pace down the street in the opposite direction than I'd been, away from the shops I knew about. After we'd walked for what seemed like four or five long city blocks and stores were getting farther apart, I thought she was taking me the wrong way.

"Kimiko, please, slow down a little. You're walking too fast for me."

"Dai-jobu," she said and slowed her pace a little.

"How much farther do we have to go?"

"Mo sukoshi. Maybe five minutes."

"But you said it was only five minutes when we left home," I said, trying not to frown.

"You walked sukoshi slow, I sink."

The twinkle in her eyes and her facial muscles struggling to keep her from grinning tattled she wasn't being disrespectful, just teasing. And I'd been led to believe that Japanese didn't have a sense of humor.

"Okay," I said, laughing. "I'll try to keep up with you. Just find that store."

After walking about eight long blocks, she turned right, leading me up what looked like a little narrow, dusty pathway. Rounding a corner I saw ahead of us small shop after shop jammed up against each other on both sides of the street. The narrow street was bulging with people mostly in native attire. Not only was the street used by pedestrians, but also by bicycles and any other vehicles that were narrow enough or brave enough to venture down it. I stuck as close to Kimiko as I could for fear of being lost or run over, not even bothering to look in the stores. I didn't see a single American among this throng, only Japanese. My height (five-feet-three) and being American made me stick out like a sore thumb. What had I let myself in for? What if these people resented an American? Kimiko must have misunderstood me and was taking me on a wild goose chase.

Tugging at Kimiko's coat sleeve, I whispered, "Kimiko, let's forget about the curtain rods. Let's go home. I'll get some someplace else."

If she was aware of my fright she didn't let on. "Mo sukoshi, I sink." she said and kept right on walking with me cowering at her side.

She entered a little dark shop and started talking to a Japanese woman who kept looking at me, and they continued speaking in Japanese for what seemed like a long time. Ill at ease, having no idea what they were saying and feeling as though my soul was bared to the world, I started looking around the store to hide my discomfort. It was a hardware store of sorts and I found some little long springs I could use. Handing them to Kimiko, together with some yen, I told her I wanted to buy them. She took care of business and, after another lengthy conversation of which I again seemed to be the subject, we departed. Almost trotting to keep up with her, I didn't complain. I just wanted to get out of there and back home.

Kimiko produced Pappa-san with some screws, and he installed my new curtain rods. Mrs. Ley and little two-year-old Nancy stopped in to check on me and, seeing what I was trying to do, offered me her assistance and the use of her sewing machine. With all of us working, we got Bonnie's bedroom curtains shortened, pressed and hung.

The next few days settled down into a repetitious routine. Seeing Bill off to work on the early morning bus, trying to instill in Bonnie more interest about school, and then restlessly waiting for the hours to go by until they returned. I just had nothing to do. My only reprieves from the monotony were the daily coffee breaks with Mrs. Ley and riding the bus to the commissary, mainly to get accustomed to the schedules and being on my own.

To simulate a Christmas spirit I didn't have, I purchased a small pine tree, which Bonnie trimmed; and in recognition of her birthday, our Friday evening supper was topped off by a "store-bought" cake, which I decorated with colored icing and added ten candles. But somehow the evening lacked the usual gaiety of a birthday celebration, even with the presents and a surprise gift from Kimiko.

Faye picked up Bonnie and me early Saturday morning to spend the day with them, and Bonnie had a wonderful time with Glenda, Pam and little Van, her three children. Bonnie went to ballet class with Glenda, and the children went to a movie. Faye and I leisurely toured the PX and I enjoyed soaking up the steam heat in their quarters.

The layout of Johnson Air Force Base and the construction of the quarters and buildings was like a little bit of America tucked away in the middle of Japan. Bill arrived in time to join us for supper and to accompany us home. However, Faye and Van talked us into staying all night as they had to attend a cocktail party, and since it was their maid's night off, we consented to stay with the children. Bonnie and Bill enjoyed themselves, but I had the feeling I was being taken advantage of, plus I didn't like not being back in my own place. After a late breakfast they drove us back to our little house and insisted we spend Christmas day with them.

The following week was filled with nothing but trouble. We ran out of gas one morning and since there was no extra bottle, Bill had to leave for work without any breakfast or hot coffee. The one time I was really loaded down with two heavy sacks of groceries the bus driver didn't stop until about two blocks past our house. My inexperience at coping with the complexities of shopping for Christmas presents left my nerves frazzled. And on top of everything else I developed a horrible cold. Apparently the steam heat at Faye's had been too warm for me, and my head felt as big as a barrel.

Bill's office was having a Christmas party and it would be my first meeting with the wives of his co-workers, and me with watery eyes and a red, runny nose. But pneumonia or not, I took a hot bath in our cold bathroom, washed my hair, and then went to bed to get warm and rest up for the long evening. Then I dressed in my best outfit, and we took the long bus ride downtown. During the bus ride Bill's alarm in his wristwatch went off loud and clear, startling everyone, that I could have crawled under the seat to avoid their humiliating stares.

A lovely buffet supper was served. The table was centered with a large ice carving of a Santa Claus, surrounded by roast beef, ham, sliced turkey, rolls, relishes, and all sorts of other good things to eat. After a floor show, a good Japanese band played for dancing. It was so nice to get out on the dance floor with Bill so I could talk to him privately.

"What in the world is wrong with me?" I asked him immediately. "Is my nose too red? Why are all those women staring at me so?"

"Relax, honey. You're the newest arrival from the States and they just want to look at what you're wearing to see what the latest style is."

"Boy, they're sure looking at the wrong person," I said. "I made this black velveteen suit and I wouldn't say it's the latest fashion."

"You look wonderful to me. Don't worry about them."

Ill at ease among strangers, I drank more cocktails than usual and, due to my cold I got just a little bit high. We did dance a lot, though, and I enjoyed myself as Bill was a superb dancer.

I was surprised to see so many Japanese girls at the party as guests of American men, but I had to admire them. Their shiny black hair was beautifully coiffed and they were dressed in brightly colored kimonos with matching zoris. I never did figure out how they danced the mambo and swing without their kimonos flying open and yet managed to look so dainty, delicate and lady-like.

16

Christmas Eve was awfully lonesome with just the three of us. We went through the rituals, but we just didn't have the Christmas spirit. We exchanged our gifts to each other, had a couple of boxes we received from the States, and we were all surprised to find that Kimiko had left a pair of fancy red Geisha-girl zoris with little bells in the heels for Bonnie, and had gotten Bill and me each a pottery beer mug with the handle in the shape of a nude girl.

Christmas morning was colder than bloody-blue-hell. The sun wasn't shining, the wind was blowing like crazy. I thought we'd never find a cab driver who could understand English enough to follow Bill's directions to Van's house. When we finally arrived at Johnson Air Force Base, the cab wasn't allowed on the base so we had to walk from the gate. It was only about three blocks, but the wind cut right through us and we were half frozen when we arrived.

After thawing out, we devoured the delicious traditional Christmas dinner of turkey and all the trimmings. A relaxing afternoon was spent looking at their home movies and colored slides of Japan, drinking egg nog, meeting their friends who dropped in, and finally them driving us home that evening.

The afternoon of December 26, Major Ley dropped in and insisted we come over to their house for some belated Christmas cheer. The way he made a drink you'd think the mix was rationed. Their affability and hospitality were so genuine we accepted their invitation to stay for supper. Jeanne's cold turkey sandwiches and leftovers were absolutely yummie.

The next day three lonesome sergeants, whose wives hadn't arrived yet from the States, stopped by for a short visit and, among other things, told us they'd heard rumors we should be in quarters by spring. That sounded good to me. If I could just stand that little house and all its inconveniences for a few more months. At least it was something to look forward to.

A couple of days later the Ley's heater conked out and Mrs. Ley and the children spent an entire evening with us to stay warm while Bill and the major tore their heater down, cleaned it and put it back together. Since trouble and hardships weren't related to rank, our mutual problems were bringing us closer together, and for the rest of my days I will be eternally grateful to Jeanne for being undaunted by my refusals to her invitations to join her, but she'd continue asking me until I accepted.

While I was still struggling with myself trying to get adjusted to the adversities and loneliness, I received a letter from my sister really scolding me for my disgruntled attitudes and feeling sorry for myself. She reminded me that we had a lot to be thankful for—we were together as a family instead of separated; that the ocean voyage alone was the envy of many who would never have such an opportunity; and that I should make every effort to learn and see all I could so I could share it with our friends back home who would never experience living in a foreign land.

So with June's scolding and Mrs. Ley's help, I made a New Year's resolution that I would try to turn over a new leaf and do better, not only for myself but more importantly for Bonnie and Bill.

17

Kimiko arrived one morning all smiles, trying to hide something behind her back. She sashayed around me and backed into Bonnie's bedroom. I had no idea what she was up to, whether I was to play along with her new "game" or just ignore her. I could hear she and Bonnie whispering and giggling, and then they both came out and handed me a package, saying, "Present-o."

"What's this? What is it for?" It wasn't my birthday, or any special day that I knew of.

"Just a present-o for you, Oku-san," Kimiko answered, still smiling.

My curiosity was aroused and I hastily undid the string and tore off the wrapping paper. I could hardly believe my eyes. The present was a penciled sketch of Bonnie on a sheet of drawing paper.

"My husband do. He sukoshi no good, but he hope you like."

"It's very good, Kimiko. But when did he ever see Bonnie?"

"Mommie, he didn't. Remember, the night Kimiko stayed with me when you and Daddy went to the party? She asked me for a picture and told me not to tell you. And this is the surprise!"

Kimiko's husband sketched as a hobby. He'd done the drawing from a billfold-size picture, yet he'd captured Bonnie's features accurately.

"We'll have to buy a frame for it," I told them. "I'm very proud of this, Kimiko, and I thank you very much."

Noting something on the back, I turned it over and read the following handwritten message:

"Bonnie-chan. Please will you pardon me.
I couldn't draw your picture very well, though
I think you are a pretty girl more than the picture,
as I am heard from Kimiko always. I most
sincerely hope you will grow up to be beautiful
and be able to get the happiness ever.
Good by pretty Bonnie-chan.
– Y. Narushima"

Reading his tender, labored-over words brought tears to my eyes. Kimiko's husband was studying English in college so he could read and write it; but she couldn't read it, only speak it.

We bought a bamboo frame for the picture, hung it up for all to see, and it became one of our most cherished mementos of Japan.

Kimiko sensed Bonnie was lonesome during her school vacation. She would hurry through her work so she would have some time to play with Bonnie. They soon discovered that if Kimiko would sweep the nap of the carpet all one way, and then use the eraser end of a pencil to draw on the rug in the opposite direction, they could make the outlines for hopscotch. Kimiko enjoyed playing this game as much as Bonnie.

She also taught Bonnie how to play a sort of shuttlecock that the Japanese play particularly around New Year's. The paddles, or hogita, are long and narrow, with brightly painted Japanese figures; and the "birdie" is made of some kind of little hard seed about the size of a pea with three small feathers attached. Although usually played outdoors without a net, they managed to play it inside.

On days when the weather wasn't too bad to be outside, Bonnie got acquainted with a little neighbor Japanese boy, Yorgi-san, the son of a tailor; and Chico-san, the daughter of a newspaper family who lived next door. Although there was a language barrier, it certainly wasn't apparent in watching them play.

From them Bonnie learned a game of skill where two children held two long bamboo poles down near the ground and clicked them together in rhythm while the third child jumps in and out of the poles without getting their ankles cracked. In turn, Bonnie taught them how to play hide-and-seek and tag. Sometimes Ley's children would join in the games, and once in a while a couple of other little Japanese girls joined them. Bonnie learned about the custom of the Japanese children relieving their bladders outdoors. She accepted it as their way of life, but never copied it.

The one game that the children all seemed to love, and one that Kimiko and Bonnie played often and I joined in, was Jan-Ken-Don—the scissors-paper-stone game that is played with one's hands and is more or less an international pastime for children of all ages. The players make a fist and say, "Jan-Ken-Don." Then each player either sticks out two fingers, opens the hand wide, or keeps it closed in a fist. The two fingers, representing scissors, can cut the paper; the open hand or "paper" can wrap the stone; and the fist or "stone" can break the scissors. It can be played as a game, used to pick a winner, or just plain fun.

Kimiko's gifts, her efforts to learn to do her work to please me, and her concern and gentleness with Bonnie made me ashamed of myself. No wonder I'd been so unhappy. I'd never been one to sit around and twiddle my thumbs. Spurred on by my resolution to do better and with Kimiko so willing, I decided to have her tell me about Japan.

Directly across from our house was a quite large building

in comparison with all the other buildings in our neighborhood. The roof was gabled and tiled, and it had an immensely tall smokestack.

"Kimiko, what is that building across the street?" I asked one day.

"That Japanese bathhouse."

Oh, ho. Then this must be one of those public bathhouses I'd heard so much about. "Is it really true that everyone takes a bath in the same tub? Tell me what it's really like?"

She explained that many Japanese were too poor to have their own bath tubs in their homes, so these public bathhouses were all over Japan, usually recognizable by the extra tall smokestacks. Men, women and children all went there. Each person takes his own towel, soap, and sometimes a wash basin. Inside the entrance were little cubbyholes in which to store their getas. Then the men go to one side, the women and children to the other side. Everyone undresses, neatly folding their clothes in a little pile. Using their own basin, they soap and scrub themselves thoroughly, rinse all the dirty, soapy water off, after which they submerge themselves neck deep in a large pool of water that is heated to almost boiling temperature. Sitting there in that hot water, they soak for an hour or more. (No wonder I'd seen people coming out of there with feet as red as lobsters. I don't know what kept them from getting pneumonia with their pores open from soaking so long, and then going out in the cold winter air barefooted.)

She said they did have a slight partition that cut off the view from either side while bathing; but they all get in the same tub of water to soak. A boy-san or girl-san, sitting on a high chair at one end, could see everyone and see whether they washed their hair, which cost an additional ten yen for women and five yen for men. Morever, if anyone had trouble washing their own back, it was possible to hire a boy-san or girl-san to scrub it.

"You go bathhouse with me sometime, Oku-san? I no sink Amelicans get crlean—wash in dirty water in tub, hai?"

"No thanks, Kimiko. I don't think I'll try it."

"If you do, I sink more better you go with me," she went on. "One time I see Amelican lady in bathhouse. It taku-san funny. Japanese women . . . how you say?" and she squatted down, "and keep head sukoshi down, and try to . .. how you say?" and she crossed both arms over her bosom, "but Amelican lady, after she wash, she just stand up and she walk like a man, swinging her arms and taking long steps to go to water. It taku-san funny. She no like Japanese woman."

She told me they keep the bathhouse open longer hours at the end of the year so everyone would have an opportunity to get clean for the New Year. They also believed in cleaning their houses that time of year and police or inspectors check to see that it is done. (This housecleaning was required twice a year.) Another custom was to have all their bills paid in full by the New Year. These were good New Year's resolutions for anyone, but I wouldn't particularly care having someone enforce them.

With Kimiko explaining local customs, I became interested in learning more about Japan. One thing bothered me, though. I was afraid I would have trouble remembering everything, plus I was sure that some things would be unbelievable unless I had some kind of proof, like pictures. I'd never been a camera bug and only knew how to operate a little Brownie box camera. Our 35-mm camera had so many little gizmos and gadgets—I skimmed through the instructions, thought I knew enough and, trusting the rest to luck, took several pictures of our house and the bathhouse. There being no other interesting subjects within range of our front yard, my enthusiasm cooled down quickly.

18

A friend drove Bill to Yokohama to pick up our car. As the day wore on I began to be a little worried. The early evening noises sounded unusually close and at the same time Kimiko was scurrying around locking the front door and checking the locks on the windows. Just as I started to ask her what she was doing, someone pounded on our front door. She motioned me to be quiet.

The pounding continued, growing stronger. I thought sure the bolt would give way, or the door would break in it looked so flimsy and shaky. Loud Japanese voices and weird music seemed to be coming through all the cracks in the house and drum beating was so loud and near it was deafening. I was so scared I was almost afraid to breathe.

The ruckus finally diminished. My curiosity overpowered my fear and I peeked out the window to see what had created this furor. Going down our steps toward the street were three Japanese men attired in wild, bizarre costumes. One had on a huge Chinese lion head, the hinged jaws snapping fiercely, and the rest of his body was covered with a brown and yellow/orange spotted material. The other two were attired in ordinary laborer or farmer clothes—navy blue, hip length, long sleeved Happi coats, blousy knicker-like pants; and black leggings. Tied around their heads were strips of white printed material, and their faces were painted a pasty white with a few colored splotches dabbed on. One was beating a small drum, another playing a reed instrument of some kind, and all three were cavorting to the rhythm of their strange music.

These were the Shisi-Mai, or Devil Dancers, who roam through the city and towns during the New Year season and rid their cash customers of the evils that cause colds, pains and aches, and bring good luck for the coming year. Kimiko explained that if she had not locked the door they would have come on in uninvited and proceeded with their devil chasing and dancing, snapping the jaws at our heads, until we paid them some yen. She said they meant no harm, they were just poor farmers trying to make a little extra money, but she thought that since I didn't know about them I would have been scared.

Oh, how right she was! It was frightening enough just listening to them trying to get in. I don't know what I would have done if they'd come in the house. I was so pleased with Kimiko. To think that she knew me well enough in this short of time she'd saved me from this harrowing experience. Bill had really done a good job when he picked her.

19

All of MAAG-J non-coms and their wives were invited to Sgt. and Mrs. McCollum's home for a New Year's Eve party. Feeling secure in our own car with Bill driving, and not able to do any sightseeing at night, I questioned him about the various people, trying to get each one clear in my mind. He got lost.

"I don't know where I'm turning wrong," he said after a while. "But I can't find their place at night. I've been there a couple of times, but it was during the daytime. It's so darned dark I can't recognize any of the landmarks or read any of the signs. Would you mind too much if we just skip the party tonight and go on home?"

"No, I don't mind." I didn't get to get dressed up very often, but I didn't know what else to say.

"I'm sorry. But there'll be other parties we can go to. I still can't figure out what I'm doing wrong."

"It's okay," I said, feeling a little disappointed as I'd hoped to become better acquainted with some of the wives. In the past we'd always developed a camaraderie with the fellas he worked with and their wives. Not wanting him to know of my disappointment, I just stared out of the car window, not really seeing anything. Suddenly I said and pointed ahead. "Look at that big rock. It's almost in the middle of the road."

"Well, I'll be damned," Bill said, driving real slow. "That's what I've been looking for. Look, can you read those signs hanging up there on that tree? Isn't their name on it somewhere?"

"But I thought we were on our way home," I said and strained to read the sign. "Yes, there's their name."

"Well, since we're here, even if it is late, we might as well go to the party for a little while," he said and swung up the narrow lane to their large, rambling Japanese style home. "But since it's so late and it took so long to get here, we won't stay very long, okay?"

The party was well under way. We were welcomed by all, and drinks were thrust into our hands. Hours later, and after much eating, drinking and chit-chat in crowded, smoke-filled rooms (a typical drunken New Year's Eve party), we finally got home about 4 a.m.

I gave up any plans of making close friends with any of them. I couldn't remember anyone individually—between the booze and the dim lights, and the horrible hung-over headache. Anyhow, the GI busses didn't go to those out of the way places.

Part III

Life in Japan

20

After the holidays, Bonnie got a desk at school and was slowly making a few friends. When the wintry weather was too miserable to be outside, I kept busy working on an embroidered appliquéd quilt, a most rewarding pastime. Even Pappa-san, who hadn't paid much attention to me one way or another, became interested in my sewing and stopped in each day to check on my progress. Kimiko told me that neither she nor Pappa-san knew that American women could sew.

My education about Japan didn't progress as rapidly as I thought it should, mainly because I didn't know intelligent questions to ask. The Stars & Stripes (published by Service personnel) and the Mainichi News (a Japanese newspaper published in English) contained a wealth of information and I started a scrapbook of interesting articles which ended up in five volumes.

I took some pictures available around our place—Bonnie waiting with the other children for the school bus; Japanese children walking by to school, with their books strapped to their backs; the red and white plaid futons (nothing more than cotton-filled thin mattresses laid on the floor for sleeping) hanging out on the wooden fences being aired daily; and the first snowfall. When my first roll of film was returned, Bill and I both were pleased with the results, and he instructed me on how to improve the quality of the pictures. Then we planned a trip that would give me the opportunity to practice what he'd taught me.

Bill's dad was stationed in Japan. He'd arrived several months before I did and was stationed at Oppama, an Army base near Yokohama. Bill hadn't seen him for sometime and, with our car, it would be a nice trip to go visit him. Fortunately, the weather wasn't too bad that Sunday. Not exactly sure of how to get there or how long it would take, we left very early that morning, loaded down with maps of Tokyo and Japan, all the camera equipment, and some snacks for the trip.

Familiar with the roads from driving to work, Bill got us to downtown Tokyo where all the main highways merged. With our maps and the few English signs posted along the highways, we succeeded in finding the road to Yokohama. The traffic hazards didn't upset me as much now and, trusting Bill's expert driving, I almost pressed my nose against the window to see all the sights.

I particularly enjoyed watching the Japanese policemen. These traffic cops were dressed in dark blue uniforms that gave them a military air. They stood on little square boxes about 18 inches square, whistles in their mouths, shoulders back and standing straight as ramrods, they would blow their whistles and wave outlandish signals with their arms stretched out full length—performing on that little box in the midst of traffic as perfect as a prima ballerina. They didn't even blink an eyelash when a vehicle brushed their coattails.

The most confusing thing about driving in Japan was making a turn off a main street crossing trolley tracks. The trolleys had the right of way, not stopping for anything except their regular stops. I couldn't figure out which was the front end of the trolley and which was the rear, plus the befuddlement of traveling on the left side of the road. I just knew I never would drive in that downtown traffic, or anywhere else in Japan for that matter.

The drive from Tokyo to Yokohama was mostly through

rolling farm land dotted with some factories and a few remaining scars from the bombings of World War II. However, the highway was a fairly new one and it proved to be a very pleasant trip.

Yokohama's heavy traffic was very much like Tokyo's except, it being an international port, the main thoroughfares were well marked in English. The road to Oppama was a very scenic drive. We could see ships coming and going to the port as we wound our way down a little narrow road along the very edge of the bay. This road was almost completely torn up for repairs and next to impossible to drive on without being bounced out of the car. Up over trolley tracks, down in a hole, then up over a sidewalk of sorts, and then a stretch of halfway decent road. Progress was quite slow, as often we had to wait our turn to use what little road was passable, or proceed so slowly because of the ruts. Bicycles and even pedestrians were passing us.

I was flabbergasted seeing that most of the workers were women, squatting and chipping away on the stones by hand with a little instrument of some kind, and very carefully fitting the stones together to form a cobblestone road. At this slow rate, even with the many laborers they had, it would surely take years to build even a short highway.

The tide was out and many, many Japanese men, women and children were wading in the bay, digging for oysters I assumed, and a few were in row boats. A little further on a myriad of bamboo frames were sticking up out of the water and lined up between the road and the bay. These frames held little square mats, approximately 12 by 14 inches, in the center of which was some greenish-black nondescript substance that was apparently drying in the sun. It was all very interesting to see, even if I didn't understand it, and I had a field day taking pictures. (Later, I learned this was seaweed caught on the frames when the tide goes out, and then dried in the sun. It's quite a delicacy for the Japanese; however, I didn't try eating it, nor did I have any desire to. It didn't even look edible to me, let alone delectable).

Still following the bay road, mountainous terrain seemed to descend on us, the mountains disappearing right into the water. The road became much more winding and we were going through one mountain tunnel after another, but each time we emerged we could see the bay. The mountains were terraced and, particularly fascinated by this terraced farming, I noticed what looked like holes or caves. Bill explained they were caves, connected with a virtual honeycomb of tunnels or passageways inside the mountains, some even as low as the roadway. Some of the lower level caves were boarded up so as not to get filled with litter and trash, but others were open and looked as though they might still be used, or at least maintained in a usable condition.

On a tour of the base we saw one of the caves, completely equipped with supplies and vehicles, and maintained by our government for an emergency hospital. This network of tunnels in the mountainous coastline regions had been built by the Japanese during World War II and inhabited by troops, supplies and artillery—no wonder they had been able to withstand so many of our attacks during the war.

The base at Oppama, primarily a U.S. Marine Base with a few Army Ordinance people, was small and we had no trouble locating Bill's dad, who was most surprised and pleased to see us. We lunched at the Service Club, checked out the local shopping district and spent considerable time in the largest shop loaded with typical souvenir items: Red and blue satin embroidered Oriental pajamas, robes and pillows; all types of Japanese dolls; metal cigarette lighters, ash trays and so on with scenes of Mt. Fuji or bamboo painted or etched on them; colored slides from all over Japan; ivory made up into jewelry and knick-knacks; and many items of brass and silver.

Just outside the back gate when we returned to the base were laborers on strike. They were congregated around an old building, some were walking back and forth with signs, some just standing around, and others sitting or sprawled on the ground. Many bright red flags and banners covered with Japanese printing and the Communist insignia were abundantly displayed. Bill's Dad told us the Communist infiltrated labor union had been causing a lot of trouble.

Although it was only about sixty miles to Oppama, it had taken us four hours to make the trip. A little weary from the long day, Bonnie stretched out on the back seat for a nap on the way home and I tried to help Bill watch for people, traffic and the right roads.

As we neared Tokyo her lights were coming on and, like any big, bustling city, the white and colored lights, some blinking, some constant, created a glow in the sky that could be seen for miles. Driving through downtown Tokyo I was fascinated by the artistic and unique way the buildings were decorated, outlined, or nearly solidly covered with colored lights. The advertising signs were ingenious and amusing. All of this glitter of electricity plus the throngs of people milling around in their native dress, with a goodly mixture of western styles, completely transformed the city from an ordinary drab, dirty city into a giant, kaleidoscopic fantasy in color.

21

To become more familiar with using the camera and so I would have a complete set of pictures from out time in Japan, the following week I busied myself with taking pictures of the various buildings at Grant Heights: The commissary, theater, chapel, Bonnie's school, and the old Zero hangars on the housing area which had been a Japanese airfield during the War. These little Zero hangars, just big enough for one small plane, were constructed partially underground and covered with sod so that from the air they would appear to be part of the terrain. They were widely scattered so a bomb wouldn't destroy all of them at once in case of an air attack.

Of course I had to get some pictures of the "honey buckets," large wooden buckets varying in size from two-and-a-half gallons to five gallons in capacity, contained the undiluted human excreta or "night soil" collected from the houses in cities and towns. These buckets are transported to farms on wagons, small three-wheeled trucks, two-wheeled pushcarts, or carried on A-frames. The everlasting parade of them by our house was as common and unnoticed to the natives as our seeing tractors or trucks back home. Needless to say, the few pictures I took of them were from a safe distance, as the smell was repulsive.

The day a scroungy, black bull pulling a wagon loaded with dirt stopped near our house, I asked Kimiko, "How come he uses a bull to pull his wagon instead of a horse?"

"I sink she sukoshi no good cow," Kimiko replied. "She boy-cow. No give milk. She has to work."

As they left, the boy-san walked by the head of the bull leading him by the halter rather than riding in the wagon and driving him with reins.

Another time a Japanese man was working on something at the neighboring house, and I asked Kimiko about it.

"He mend tatami," she told me. It looked so interesting. In a squatted position he was sewing on this straw mat and I wanted a closer look. "Do you think he would mind if I took his picture while he works?"

"I don't sink so."

"Will you go down with me and ask him if he would let me take his picture?"

"Hai, I go."

Kimiko spoke to him in Japanese, he answered her, and she turned to me, saying, "He speak daijobu. He speak many Amelicans take his picture."

The man went on with his work as I took his picture, and then with a slight nod of the head, faced me with a friendly smile.

Kimiko was the solution to my dilemma. I would have her accompany me and be my interpreter. I wasn't certain how to approach these people, and I definitely didn't want to offend anyone. And I wouldn't have to go out alone.

One evening Bonnie came running into the house, "Mom, quick, let's go see the man with the balloons," she said and excitedly grabbed my hand, tugging me to follow her. "He's got all kinds. Maybe I could get one, huh, could I, huh?"

"Where is he?" I asked, looking for the camera.

"Just down the street a little ways. I saw him from the bus. Hurry, Mom, before he leaves."

"C'mon, Kimiko."

As we all dashed out the front door, Bill was coming up our steps.

"Whoa, there," he said. "Where's everyone going in such a hurry?"

"Daddy, see down there? We're going down to see the balloon man."

"Well, how about that. Care if I go, too?"

The balloon man was parked about half-way between our house and Grant Height's entrance. A dozen or more balloons tied to his push-cart whipped about in the air as though trying to break their ties. He had mammoth red round balloons, long green balloons, and yellow ones shaped like an octopus. Bill bought a big octopus-shaped balloon for Bonnie and, pointing on down the street, said, "Look, Bonnie, there's someone selling birds. Shall we go see that, too?"

"Oh, yes, yes, Daddy. Let's go!"

And off they went, with Kimiko and me following. A little, old wizened lady, back slightly bent, with thin, long stringy hair flowing from her head, had a cartload of wooden and metal bird cages, each imprisoning a different kind or color of bird.

"Daddy, can I have a bird?" Bonnie pleaded.

"Oh, I don't know about that."

"Please, Daddy, you won't let me have a dog. Can I, please, have a bird? Daddy, purrty puleese?" she said, looking lovingly at him and patting him.

"Well, let's look them over and we'll see."

I stood back to take some pictures. Bill and Kimiko were looking at the birds and talking to the sales lady. Squinting through the view finder, I saw Bonnie all smiles, holding up a green metal cage with a little yellow canary in it.

"Don't worry, Mom," Bill told me. "The cage and canary both only cost me a little less than 1800 yen (approximately $5) and Kimiko can help Bonnie take care of him."

At that price, why argue? I thought.

"Tweedie Pie" entertained us for the remainder of our stay in Japan with the most beautiful singing I've ever heard. Pappa-san told me he was an inchi-ban canary except for the little black mark on top of his head. He took charge of caring for Tweedie Pie, bringing fresh greens every day, clipping his nails, and seeing that he got the proper diet and fresh air.

22

Answering a knock on the door one day, an American GI told me: "We have your furniture down here. We'll unload it and put it here in front of your house, if that's okay."

My gosh, the furniture I'd shipped from the States. I'd almost forgotten about it. I'd shipped it several weeks before I left and we'd been in Japan now for a couple of months. Seeing the big Army van parked in the parking lot, I got that sinking feeling. Our little house was full already, and I was reminded of the very short list of things Bill had told me to bring and thought of all the things I'd had shipped. And there they all were, stacked in front of our house. I stared at that big pile of crates—it looked bigger than our house! What was I going to do? I needed help, so I went next door to the Ley's.

"Jeanne, look out there," I said, pointing to the crates. "Will you tell me what I'm going to do with all that stuff?"

"Good heavens, Geil, what'd you do—ship everything you own?

"No, not quite. Just what I thought we'd need to make our place seem more like home," I answered her guiltily.

"Well, let's find Pappa-san so he can start uncrating the stuff."

Kimiko was so anxious to see what was in all of the boxes she'd found Pappa-san and was happily fixing us coffee and cinnamon toast. Pappa-san broke open the crates, carefully saving all the nails and sorting the wood pieces by size.

"What am I going to do, Jeanne? Bill wrote and told me to bring some rugs, a stove and refrigerator combination, a wringer type washing machine—and look what's out there. If I don't get those things all put away before he comes home tonight, he'll go straight through the roof."

"Don't worry, Geil. We'll figure out something. After all, with you and me, with Kimiko's and Pappa-san's help, we'll get everything under control somehow."

How stupid I'd been not to follow Bill's instructions to the letter. Here we had nice, comfortable government furniture and I'd shipped all our old things. But there just wasn't time to sit around feeling sorry for myself and worrying about what Bill would say. I had to get busy and get something done.

Starting in our bedroom, we moved out one of the GI dressers, then laid the two gray rugs, added a small blond buffet, console type sewing machine and a large thread box. We took all of the GI furniture out of Bonnie's bedroom, covered the floor with bright red rugs, set up her bed, dresser, a desk and chair, steamer trunk, and cedar chest with a dollhouse on top. The bathroom was big enough for the washing machine, tub and bucket, plus the ironing board, vacuum cleaner and dirty clothes hamper. Out went the two upholstered GI chairs, table and straight chairs from the living room, and we squeezed in a daybed, lounge chair with large ottoman, an upholstered green plastic chair, dinette table with four chairs, one end table and table lamp, a record player, cabinet and records, plus a floor electric fan. The GI refrigerator was shoved from the kitchen into the living room. The stove-refrigerator combination was installed in the corner of the kitchen.

We practically had wall-to-wall furniture. All the extras, such as Bonnie's bike, footlockers, etc., had to be stored outside on the concrete slab in front of the house. Pappa-san found some bamboo to curtain them from view and from the weather.

It was a hard, back-breaking day's work, but we were proud of our accomplishments, except ... we still had a problem. We had two end tables and a table lamp of ours left over, and all the GI furniture was now stacked outdoors. Since it was either rainy or threatening rain most of the time, it couldn't be left outside.

Bless Jeanne. She offered to take our extra furniture. Then she drove me over to Supply and I told them of my problem. Surprisingly, a truck was immediately sent out and picked up the government furniture.

Kimiko was pleased with all the new arrivals, but disappointed that I didn't have some photographs of the States and of our family and friends. She could hardly wait to try out the washing machine. She'd been doing part of our laundry by hand, and the rest we had been sending out to a nearby laundry.

That evening as Bill comfortably relaxed in his own chair, with his shoes off and his feet propped up on the foot stool, he chided me about my foolishness in having shipped so many things. But since it was done and nothing could be done about it, he had to admit it seemed pretty nice having our own furniture.

23

A school friend of Bonnie's also lived in private rental away from other Americans. Since both girls missed English-speaking playmates of their own age, we had Donna over one afternoon after school. I've never seen two happier little girls as they played with Bonnie's dolls. The time flew for all of us. After we finished supper it was time to drive Donna home.

Houses in Japan had an address, but instead of a street name and house number the address consisted of a house number (assigned when the house was built, not according to its location on a particular street), the prefecture, railroad station and city. For example, our address was 282 Kamiakatsu-cho Machi (prefecture), Itabashi-ku (railroad station), Tokyo, Japan. The house right next to us had the same address, except their house number was 1415. It was practically impossible to locate a particular place by an address alone—even the Japanese postmen had trouble.

Consequently, Donna's father had drawn us a map showing exactly how to get to their house, and we had little trouble following its markings. We'd never met Donna's parents and she insisted we meet her mother.

Their private rental was a big Japanese style home, completely surrounded by a high wooden fence. Immediately inside the outer sliding wooden doors was a small foyer for removing one's shoes before stepping up approximately eighteen inches to the interior of the house.

"Mother," Donna called out. "I'm home, and Bonnie's folks are with me."

Donna's mother appeared from the back of the house, invited us in and told us to leave our shoes on or our feet would get cold. They had wooden floors and not tatami.

"Thank you so much for having Donna over. She's been so lonesome with no Americans around here. C'mon, I'll give you a quick tour of the house on our way to the kitchen. It's a mess, but it's the only warm room in the house."

All of the rooms were quite large with high ceilings and opened off of a long central hall. The full-length sliding doors and windows opening to the outside were constructed of wood and thin glass, the inside ones made of rice paper. The cold wind was blowing in, through and under the house, and they were trying unsuccessfully to heat this barn-like of a place with only two coal-burning, pot-bellied tent stoves.

To preserve what little heat there was, the bedrooms and

extra rooms were closed off. Each bedroom contained a Japanese hibachi, or earthenware brazier, to take the chill out of the air when the room was being used.

Our untimely arrival caught Mrs. Byrd and her houseboy in the dirty job of trying to clean the flues. One pipe, about eight feet long, had become so clogged it had pulled apart and dumped soot all over one end of the kitchen. My heart ached for her as she brushed at the soot trying to clean a place for us, apologizing about her dirty kitchen. Soon, though, we were visiting like old friends.

She thanked us again for having Donna over, and particularly for coming in for a visit. She confessed that prior to our arrival her spirits had been so low that the soot catastrophe had about been the straw that broke the camel's back. Our arrival and visit had been a lifesaver. This made me feel horribly ashamed of the way I'd been acting since my arrival in Japan. Our living conditions were luxurious compared to hers, and she was a major's wife.

Ready to go home, we discovered the street was too narrow in which to turn the car around. To complicate matters, on either side of the road was a deep ditch about a foot and a half wide. By inching the car forward, and then inching it backwards, back and forth, back and forth, Bill finally made a right hand turn down another narrow road.

When we'd left our house it was early dusk, but we had visited so long the sky had darkened. It was a residential district with only a few street lights now and then and it was hard to see the little narrow road. We figured two more right turns and then a left, and we'd be on the return road and could follow the hand-made map. Each of us peered into the darkness watching for the next corner.

We made the next turn fairly easy; however, the road wasn't much wider, and instead of going straight it began winding every which way. At the very next corner it was just impossible to make a turn, right or left. Besides being narrow and having the ditches on each side, four big concrete poles were set in the street, on each corner inside the ditches, so there was nothing to do but continue following the little winding street.

Bill's untalkativeness and intense concentration on his driving sent a foreboding chill down my spine. What kind of mess had I gotten us into this time? Had I become so complacent in our little friendly neighborhood I'd forgotten we were living in nearly the largest city of the world of which we knew so little, and parts of which had absolutely no signs in English? Remembering the trouble we'd had going to Sgt. McCullom's and having read somewhere that even the U.S. Army Engineers had run into trouble trying to mark the main highways of Tokyo because there was no rhyme or reason to how the streets were laid out, the thought struck me we could get lost real easy. I kept staring out of the window, wishing for a familiar landmark to appear.

Bill disgustedly told me to forget the map. He was going to take the next wider street regardless of the direction. We traveled for quite a distance before we found one. After turning on it, we came upon a small business district that we all thought looked like the one we'd gone through on our way to Donna's. After crossing a railroad track, that Bonnie and I were positive were the ones we'd previously crossed, I sort of settled back and decided my premonition had been for naught.

Looking for a familiar clue to match up with on the map proved fruitless. We were on another winding, narrow road, and it got narrower and narrower, winding more and more, with shops built right up to the edge of the street. It was the most congested street I'd seen. The shops and street were full of people and we kept meeting bicycles that could just barely get by us. The small wattage lights from the shops cast eerie shadows everywhere. The people looked at us as though we were intruders in their private little world. Nowhere could I find any kind of a sign in English.

"Damn it," Bill said. "I'll bet I should have turned the other way off that street back there."

His swearing convinced me that we were indeed lost.

"This could be one of those damn streets that gets so narrow we may end up having to back out of here."

My heart started beating hard and fast. How could we possibly back up as far as we'd driven? I wondered. But, if we couldn't get out the other end of this road, what else could we do?

"I only hope we're in a friendly part of Tokyo and it's not one of those sections where they don't like Americans."

Ahead, a small three-wheeled truck blocked the street. Bill pulled up behind the vehicle, stopped the car and honked. No one was in or near the truck. One by one the people on the street started moving toward us, their getas clopping on the cobblestones. Bill lowered his window and called out, "Hey, Boy-san, dozo. Dozo," and he gestured for the truck to be moved.

A hissing sound emanated from the crowd. Air was being sucked through their teeth—bared in a grin or a grimace, I wasn't sure which—as they shook their heads and shrugged their shoulders. Nothing could be done. More people were appearing out of the shadows. The swelling sea of humanity shoved the front lines against our car. These people acted as though they'd never seen Americans before, just staring at us from myopic, slanted eyes.

I scooted lower in my seat, hoping to disappear, and crossed my legs to control my bladder. Pictures of torture by villainous Japanese soldiers during WWII flashed through my mind. I knew I'd never see the light of day again. I was SCARED!

How do you measure time—by the second, the minute, the hour? I had no idea. I just wanted this to end.

Lady Luck, disguised as a Japanese farmer, emerged from the crowd and drove the truck into an entryway so we could proceed.

"Dai jobu. Domo arigato, Pappa-san," Bill called out and waved a friendly salute to the driver. Ahead was a nice wide avenue. My labored breathing eased. Bill recognized the surroundings and we were soon on N Avenue headed to our little house.

One thing about that night we never did understand was that when we first turned off N Avenue going to Byrd's house we turned right and, having never crossed it at any time in all our roaming around, by any standards of reason we should have turned left when we finally reached N Avenue to be headed home (which we did and which was wrong).

So we wouldn't get in this kind of a pickle again, I got a letter off to my sister to send us a compass for our car. And the mystery still remains, as we never went back to try to solve it. After all I'd been through that night, I really appreciated our little abode and particularly its location.

Our next few motor trips were in broad daylight in familiar territory or near enough to our place that we wouldn't get lost. On one such tour into the country we asked Kimiko to accompany us.

Although spring hadn't arrived enough for the farmers to be working in the fields, it was interesting to see the patchwork quilt effect of the terraced barren fields, edged in little mounds of earth (molded out of mud by crude hoes, shaped and firmly packed by hands and feet) for the purpose of controlling the water when irrigating or flooding the rice fields. The farmers' thatched-roofed homes, usually several homes built in a group, were surrounded by either high bamboo fences or trees that had been trimmed and intertwined to form a windbreak against the cold winter winds and typhoons.

We did find one field of clover in full bloom, edged by a little stream in which several small boys were catching frogs. Bonnie asked us to stop, and she and Kimiko picked blossoms and romped through the field like a couple of young, carefree colts.

This little excursion brought back many memories for Kimiko. She told us that during the first part of the War her father had sent her and her mother to live in the country away from the danger of Tokyo being bombed. As little as she was, she had to climb mountains, cut firewood and haul it strapped to her back. She worked in the rice fields, wading bare footed through the muddy waters transplanting the tender rice shoots, her legs and arms almost covered with leaches after each day's work.

With each little facet that Kimiko revealed about herself, the less we thought of her as a maid and the more we considered her as an individual person in her own right.

24

Bill came home one evening with the bad news that MAAG-J people would no longer be on the list for quarters at Grant Heights or any other housing area. This was a real blow to me, as I'd been existing from day to day with the hope of getting to live on a dependent's housing area in government quarters so I could make more friends and live a more normal life. Now that was out of the question. He did say, though, they were planning on building new quarters for MAAG-J personnel, but so far plans hadn't been formulated.

The Leys got their bid for temporary quarters, and I could feel myself sinking back into depression. Jeanne was the only friend I'd really made, as our other neighbors either remained there a short time, or the wives worked, or we just didn't have mutual interests.

Jeanne recognized the lethargy I was getting in and insisted that since I had nothing better to do I may as well go with them to see the quarters. I thought this would only be pouring salt on my wounds but, admitting that I didn't have anything else to do and being glad for them for the chance of getting quarters, I went along with her and Major Ley just to see how the others got to live in Japan.

They could select one of two sets of quarters at Washington Heights (which was closer to downtown Tokyo and Major Ley's work), or their choice of four at Grant Heights. None of us liked the quarters at Washington Heights. They were built too close together with only a small yard; two-stories, heated by a floor furnace located at the bottom of the stairs so all the heat would go upstairs leaving the downstairs uncomfortably cold. Also, most of the VIPs (generals and full colonels of the Army and Air Force) in the Tokyo area lived in Washington Heights so there were few young children there near the ages of the Ley's children.

When Jeanne asked my opinion of the quarters, I told her I didn't like them. But then I added: "They're a lot better than where we live now. I guess the main reason I don't like them is because they're so far from where we live I'm afraid if you move here I'll never see you again."

"I don't like them either," Jeanne answered. "I'm so glad you said that, Geil. I wouldn't want to be stuck clear up here away from you with all the 'big wheels.' C'mon, Ed. Let's go see what they've got at Grant Heights. You're used to driving the distance anyhow, so it shouldn't make that much difference to you."

They selected a place at Grant Heights as temporary quarters until the availability of a three or four bedroom authorized for their family size and rank.

After the Leys moved, I felt Jeanne would be drawn into the usual activities of helping at school, making new friends, having coffee with her new neighbors, etc., and I withdrew inside myself. Mornings I would busy myself with some sewing, or help Kimiko with her work, and otherwise occupy myself so I wouldn't get too lonesome.

Kimiko asked many questions about the States and particularly what our stateside home was like. She tried to help me learn a little Japanese, but I was a very poor student. She did well in teaching Bonnie to speak and understand the language. I had neither the mental capacity nor patience to learn the various pronunciations used for the Hepburn spelling, the most commonly used system, let alone the Nippon and Kunrei spellings, which were completely different. Of course, there was the Kanji, and I don't know how many other forms of Japanese printing that just looked like chicken tracks to me, which I didn't even attempt to learn. I did acquire sufficient knowledge to help me better pronounce the few words I'd have occasion to use; and I started calling Kimiko:

"Kee-mee-ko" correctly rather than "Kim-i-ko" as I had been doing.

While sitting and sewing one day, I felt a quick prick in my head. Kimiko had pulled out a hair.

"What'd you do that for?" I asked, rubbing my head.

"Glay hair," she answered, showing me.

"Good heavens, don't do that. When you pull one gray hair, forty more will grow in its place—or I'll be bald headed."

"I don't sink so. My Mamma-san have me pull her glay hairs. She got taku-san black hair."

She told me about the first time she'd heard Americans were in Japan after the War, and how scared she was but how much she wanted to see what Americans looked like. She'd always heard we were "white" people and how surprised she was when she finally saw her first American to see that his skin wasn't white-white like paper, but, as she said, "Sukoshi-yellow, like Japanese.

"See, Oku-san, we no so different," as she placed her arm alongside of mine to compare skin colors. Even though I'm fair skinned and was without a summer tan, the color of my arm wasn't too much lighter than hers. It was hard for me to understand why we called them "yellow-skinned."

25

The sun was slowly winning its battle against the dreary, rain-filled clouds in preparation for Spring's arrival. Bonnie, Kimiko and I took advantage of the nice days by going on long, late afternoon strolls through the neighborhood. I never tired of exploring all the little neighborhood specialty shops. Shoe stores, fish stores, vegetables and fruit stores, something akin to hardware stores, pachinko parlors, coffee shops, noodle shops, material stores, sink and benjo stores, flower shops, paint stores, rattan furniture stores, china shops, souvenir shops, brass and silver shops, jewelry shops, tailors and seamstresses—congregated into little shopping districts. Some were little local markets built in the front part of homes; others catered only to Americans and the tourist trade; and some catered to the local inhabitants.

Fruits and vegetables scrubbed until they actually glistened, each and every color a deep, brilliant hue, were displayed at a "fruitier." Carrots about three or four inches in diameter and twelve inches long; apples and peaches the size of big grapefruits; strawberries almost the size of lemons, packed six to a box (similar to an egg carton); cabbages as large as watermelons; and a strange vegetable that looked like a cross between a white radish and a turnip which was about eight inches across the top and a good eighteen inches long. Kimiko called these daiku and said they were used as a basis for soups, sukiyaki, and mixed in with other cooked vegetables.

Except for some delicious fruit resembling persimmons, called kaki, I resisted the temptation to buy anything from this lavish display. The U.S. medics advised that anything grown locally underground should be boiled before eating because of the night soil or fertilizer. Besides, I'd seen vegetables scrubbed in little, dirty ditches which were also used for washing clothes and utensils, emptying garbage in and urinating in. This did make me think a lot.

The Japanese transported everything under the sun, including the kitchen sink, on their bicycles. Many such items Americans would have to hire a truck to move them. Like a full-grown tree precariously balanced on a little two-wheel cart, its branches dangling over the rider's head like mistletoe, looking as if it might tip over by the slightest bump; or several poles of bamboo approximately twenty feet long balanced on the rider's shoulders as he rode his bike with both hands on the handlebars; and a girl with a live pig sitting in a basket tied on the back of her bike.

The O-sobai-san were particularly fun to watch. These boys delivered food from restaurants to the people at work or at home. Six to eight bowls of soup or noodles on a tray, stacked several trays high, were balanced on one upraised hand and, with the other hand on the handlebars, they snaked their way through heavy traffic—over rocky dirt roads, bouncing up over curbs, and down heavily foliated paths—never spilling a drop, or hardly ever.

One afternoon Bonnie came in all excited wanting Kimiko and me to go with her. Parading up and down the street across from us were three or four Japanese dressed up in blue-and-white printed costumes, with white make-up on their faces. Each one was playing an odd instrument and one was beating on a drum. Kimiko told us they were advertising a sale at the local fish market. We visited the store and the shopkeeper offered us some octopus. I declined, but Bonnie tried it. She didn't particularly like it. It was tough and the more she chewed it the bigger it got.

Whenever a store had a sale or a new business opened, these Shindonya were hired for advertising. Huge paper flower wreaths on high easels adorned the front of their place of business. With the noise of the Shindonya and the colorful wreaths, it was impossible to miss a sale or opening. These wreaths, Hanawa, or pachinko wreaths (because of the many pachinko houses opening) were about two-and-one-half feet in diameter, mounted on easels six to eight-feet high. Friends send the Hanawa as our people send floral pieces to a new business.

The Pachinko Parlors were entertainment centers filled with pin-ball machines. The machines stood upright and, side by side, lined the walls and formed rows back to back, with just enough room in the aisles for customers to stand back to back and play them. It was a very popular pastime for Japanese as well as Americans.

Another sight that interested us was watching laborers dig a well. Down in the hole was a pappa-san filling a large wooden bucket. Several women tugged on a rope attached to a tripod with a pulley affair, pulling the dirt-filled bucket up to the surface to be emptied. Women always seemed to have the hard, back-breaking labor to do.

Buildings of all sizes were being erected all over the city.

The carpenters, using bamboo poles laced together around the structure, were as agile as monkeys climbing around this framework from which they worked. Our walks, auto rides and bus trips always produced such striking scenes, with each glimpse revealing a little more about Japan and her people.

26

Betty Gladding, a friend of Jeanne's who knew of a particular little china shop along the bus route, invited Jeanne and me to join her. What an interesting assortment of unusual shapes and designs. Not being a connoisseur of fine china, I selected only items that particularly appealed to me—a set of large, clear glass pharmaceutical-type jars with glass lids (large enough to hold five pounds of sugar or flour) for canisters; a large round fish bowl, about fourteen inches in diameter with a ten-inch opening in the top, resting on a black pedestal; and four little rice bowls, each painted with a different picture.

The store, off the beaten track of tourists, sold to the local neighborhood. The prices were very cheap and none of the items had "Made in Japan" on them as all export items are marked. How pleased I was when Kimiko told me the rice bowls were ichi-bon china because of their translucency and hand-painted designs by artists sufficiently famous to be permitted to inscribe their names.

A fish bowl without fish is just a white elephant. I'd have to get some fish. A few days later a fish salesman, with a pushcart loaded with glass containers filled with fish, went by the house. By the time I had my camera, rounded up Bonnie and got Kimiko away from her work, he had turned down a little street and we had to run several blocks to catch up with him. He had several kinds of fish, including all sizes of gold fish. Some of his gold fish were as big as river catfish. Bonnie purchased two lively small gold fish, which he put in a water-filled plastic bag for carrying.

Chasing the fishman had taken us a considerable ways off the main road, and walking back we came upon a young lad pounding two wooden sticks together. Children came running from all directions, gathering around him. Curious, I had to wait and see what was going on. Kimiko told me he was a Kami-shibai, who sold candy and gum to the children.

As the children stood fascinated, munching on their candy, this meager actor told them a story. He made it more interesting by using colored drawings, approximately twelve inches by fifteen inches, set up in a box designed like a miniature stage and arranged so he could change the pictures quickly. This make-believe stage was tied on the handlebars of his bicycle. The children watched and listened to him with the same rapture as our children view a movie or television show. Although I couldn't understand the story, it was interesting to see the painted pictures and listen to the various intonations of his voice as he portrayed the various characters of his story. We'd acquired our goldfish and some more Japanese culture.

27

Jeanne and Ed were assigned their permanent quarters on Grant Heights, a nice little separate house with three bedrooms, a large living-dining room area, bath, small kitchen and maid's room. It had a large yard where the children could play. This would be their home for the next two years, and Jeanne was interested in fixing it as attractive and livable as possible. Furniture, rugs and drapes issued by the government resulted in most quarters looking the same inside as well as out, with the exception of the color scheme. This could be a decorating problem if Supply didn't have a complete color-matched set of furnishings.

When Jeanne moved, drapes of any color were impossible to get from Supply. I suggested she should be different and make curtains for her house. Hiroko, Jeanne's new maid, told us of a big material store at Ikebukuro where we could buy almost any color or kind of material we would want at Japanese prices. We measured the windows, figured the yardages we would need and made preparations for our big shopping spree.

It was chilly and rainy the day we were to go to Ikebukuro, but as Jeanne had the car and decided she would rather try driving than struggling with packages on the bus, we were undaunted by the bad weather. Bundled up in our raincoats, rain hats and galoshes, we bravely set forth on our first farthest jaunt downtown unescorted.

Ikebukuro, about a thirty-minute drive from where we lived, had a large shopping district. We found a parking lot and joined the throngs on the sidewalks. Progress was quite an ordeal as it seemed that we were trying to go in the opposite direction of everyone else and were jostled around until we felt like a pair of punching bags. Each and every man, woman and child we met was carrying an opened umbrella, and Jeanne and I, taller than the average Japanese, were in constant fear of getting our heads knocked off or our eyes poked out by the innumerable umbrellas.

We darted under the canopy of a big department store (Saebus) to get out of the rain and out of the main pedestrian stream of traffic. Pausing here to catch our breath, we noticed some strange devices in the lobby—several big metal cans to each of which was attached a rubber hose tipped with a brush. Not in any particular hurry, we waited to find out what they were. Our wait was short. These contrivances were used to wash the mud from rubber boots, worn mostly by the Occidentilized Japanese, before entering the store. The Japanese women who still wore native attire and most of the men and boys wore special rain shoes which were wooden getas, except the two blocks of wood under the sole were about three or four inches high, permitting the wearer to walk through puddles without getting his feet wet. As we weren't sure whether this "boot-washing machine" was free or cost money, and since our boots were only wet and not muddy, we bypassed the machines and entered the store.

The interior resembled any large department store decorated for some holiday or special sale. We were out of the rain but we certainly hadn't escaped from "people." But since we were only looking around and didn't know where the different departments were, we let ourselves be carried along with the crowd—there wasn't much choice anyhow. Before we realized what was happening, we were shoved into an elevator. People kept pushing in until we were packed together tighter than sardines in a tin can.

While discussing whether to get off on the second floor, more people got in the elevator than got off, the doors were closed and we were going up. Just before reaching the third floor the elevator stalled. The operator pushed all the buttons, jiggled the controls, but we didn't move, up or down. Everyone started talking; we could feel the pulsation of muscles tensing in a desire for movement of some kind.

"Oh, my gosh, Geil, what'll we do?" Jeanne's voice was hoarse and quivering. She glanced towards the roof of the car, "Look, there isn't even an escape hatch in here."

I was so scared I was speechless. We gripped each other's hands until our knuckles were white and the veins stood out.

"Geil, if we ever get out of this alive, I'll never get in another elevator as long as I stay in Japan."

"That goes for me, too," I quickly agreed. "Let's just hope the others in here don't panic and crush us to death."

The car started quivering, then jerking and, straining under its load, gradually moved upwards. When the doors opened at the third floor, we wasted no time pushing past the others for a quick exit. Breathing deeply to calm our nerves, and thankful our worries had been worse than our experience, we browsed through the china department. This wasn't getting the curtain material, so we reluctantly searched for the stairway, and on to another store.

Braving the weather and the perils of the sidewalk again, we located Kinkidos, the material shop. The aisles were more crowded than at Saebus, but the bolts and bolts of material stacked on tables and counters beckoned irresistibly.

"If we're going to do any good in here, I guess we're going to have to push and shove our way around," Jeanne told me as she led the way.

I was averse to the idea of having to push and be aggressive as we were the foreigners. But after being poked in my ribs, squashed between mamma-sans with half-grown children strapped to their backs, my boots filled with water from dripping umbrellas, and my toes flattened by wooden getas until they felt like a bloody pulp, I got my dander up.

"I guess I can shove with the best of them or get mauled to death. Let's try to stick close together though, but in case we do get separated, I'll meet you at the front door." Then, squaring my shoulders, bracing my arms so that my skinny elbows made sharp points at either side, I forged ahead.

Edging over next to the counters, we removed our gloves and ran our fingers over the material trying to determine the content and quality. Worming our way along, we became more disheveled by the minute. Our hats were finally dislodged and we stuffed them in our pockets so as not to lose them.

"Jeanne, would you look at these people. They're all staring at us and grinning. Are we that odd looking?"

"Beats me. Maybe we'd better check our clothes and see if something's been torn off and we're indecent."

Then I noticed a lady pointing at Jeanne's head. "Hey, I think it's your hair. I don't think they've seen too many blondes."

"Oh, I'll bet that's it. Well, you're not black-headed either, you know. At least it'll be easy to find each other if we get separated. We're probably the only two people in here that don't have black hair."

"Hey, look at this," I said. I'd found a table full of some beautifully soft material in every color of the rainbow and all the colors in between. "I'm not sure what kind of material it is. It feels a little like batiste, but it's softer and more silky. But I think it would make up beautifully into cafe curtains."

"Oooh, aren't they pretty!" she said and searched through the bolts, comparing colors, and finally selected white for the living room, orange for the boys' room, and a soft, minty green for her bedroom. "Wonder what we'll have to do to get waited on? Do you suppose we can make them understand us?"

A petite Japanese girl appeared before us, bowed low, and said, "Prease, Madame?"

"You understand English?" we both asked.

"Sukoshi."

"Good. Is this cotton?" Jeanne asked her, indicating her choices. "And will it wash?"

"No cotton, 'layon. For rining kimonos. Wash okay."

We were sufficiently oriented to know that "'layon" was rayon and "rining" was lining.

"How much will it shrink?" I asked her.

"Shlink?" asked the clerk, wrinkling her brow and shaking her head. "I no understand."

Slowly, I said, "You speak wash okay?"

"Hai, wash okay."

"Okay. After wash, maybe shorter?" I said, motioning with my hands. "How much shorter?"

She looked puzzled for a moment, and then, "Hai, I understand. Maybe one inch, one yard, but wash okay."

The material was only about twenty-nine inches wide so we had to refigure the yardage. Our final figures added up to so many yards the clerk called a couple of boy-sans to go for more material. Such a large purchase must have been a rarity. Four or five clerks, talking and giggling, measured and wrapped the material while the customers just stood and stared in disbelief.

More than pleased with the price—equal to about twelve cents a yard—and with yen left and an English-speaking clerk, Jeanne bought some orange-and-white plaid material for bedspreads, and I bought some material for clothes.

Loaded down with our bundles and pleased with our purchases, we were escorted to the door by our newly acquired friend, the little Japanese clerk, who cleared the way for us. As we left the store, she handed each of us a Japanese printed hand towel and a palm leaf fan as a present-o, asking us to come again.

28

Jeanne's quarters became a second home to me during the daytime when Bill and Bonnie were gone as I helped her make the curtains and bedspreads. They became the envy of everyone who saw them and spurred us on to bigger and better decorating ideas.

Since Pappa-san, who worked at our house, was very handy in making anything by just looking at a picture, she had him construct some simple cornices for the windows and paint them a dark green. Jeanne wanted the dark green upholstered furniture she'd seen in other quarters instead of the unmatched faded light brocade they had. So we went to Supply to see about getting what she wanted. But the sergeant there advised us the green was the newest furniture and they didn't have any in stock.

"Will you take my name and call me when some green furniture is turned in?" she asked him.

"I'm sorry, Ma'am, we can't do that. It's against regulations and too many people want it."

"Okay, thanks anyway."

Out of hearing range of the sergeant, I asked Jeanne, "Can't we find someone with that furniture who's shipping out and we'll switch your furniture with them before they turn it in? Supply doesn't check the color, only the item."

"That's exactly what I was thinking. Guess I'll just have to go to some of the officers' wives coffees and get the low-down on who the short timers are."

When she'd learn of someone moving who had some furniture she wanted, we'd load one of her chairs in her station wagon, drive to the other quarters and unload her piece; load up the one she'd selected and take it back to her house. Piece by piece we traded her furniture until she had a completely matched living room set; and I'm sure we shocked the maids and house-boys when they saw American women doing such hard labor.

The PX at Camp Drake was to get a shipment of rattan chairs and tables, Jeanne learned by the grapevine, and she had her heart set on getting some. The supply being less than the demand, we arrived at the PX before it opened. I went with her just to keep her company; but after standing in line an hour and a half, I decided to get some, too, rather than sweat that line out again. I hadn't the vaguest notion where I'd put them in our already crowded house, but was still hoping we'd get government quarters and have space to use all of our furniture.

To make room for our new furniture, Jeanne, Kimiko, Pappa-san and I moved the GI bed out of our room to be returned to Supply. It took all four of us to lift just the mattress. The bed was so hard and was never comfortable, now I was sure it was stuffed with rocks.

Our daybed was moved into the bedroom for our bed. Since we were in the moving business, I pulled the sliding doors off the closet, as they were a nuisance always getting off their tracks. I couldn't throw them away and there was no place to store them, so I stood them up behind the daybed where they looked like a paneled headboard.

When we were finished, Kimiko started laughing. "I sink maybe Serlgeant wake up some night and see doors and he maybe go through wall."

The two circle saucer chairs and round rattan table added to the rearranged living room enhanced the looks of the room, and the daybed was a much more comfortable bed.

29

The last week of April the stores and shops set up displays of Japanese dolls in celebration of Hina Matsuri, or Girl's Day, celebrated on May 3. The most interesting were the exhibits showing the ideal or ultimate collection of which every Japanese girl dreams.

To help Americans have a better understanding and appreciate the true meaning of such a collection, Narimasu School had such an exhibit. Each of the dolls was labeled as to type of doll, age or origin, with specific meaning or interesting information. Several Japanese authorities on the manufacture and collection of dolls were present to answer questions. There were miniature dolls, only an inch or two high, very intricately carved and hand-painted; wooden dolls; cloth dolls; paper dolls; Kokeshi dolls; Hokata dolls; Geisha dressed dolls, ranging in size to about thirty inches high, some encased in glass boxes.

The center of attraction was the stair-step shelves, covered in rich red velvet, filled with replicas of the Imperial Court, with the Emperor and Empress on the top shelf; the lower shelves containing courtiers, warriors and palace officials, placed according to rank and precedence, and miniature furniture. There was also a quite elaborate and detailed gold replica of the Emperor's palace.

These dolls are only collector's items, as the little Japanese girls do not play with them. On Hina Matsuri they are displayed in a place of honor in the homes, then carefully stored away until the next year; and passed down from one generation to the next.

Bonnie and I became quite interested in the dolls and started a small collection. The dolls we acquired were precious to us because they were gifts from Japanese friends or reminiscent of a particular person or place.

30

One evening at the Leys, Jeanne asked the fellas what they thought of having a screen of some kind made to divide the dining room from the living room. "Why couldn't we get some Japanese wooden window or door frames, without the rice paper? Wouldn't that make a nice room divider?"

"Are you crazy or something?" Ed said quickly. "That wouldn't work. How would you make them stand up? You can't drill any holes in the wall, you know."

"I think it sounds like a good idea," I said, adding my suggestions. "We could get some small ones and set them on top of bookcases. Or, better yet, make a planter box to hold the frames, put in some plants and train the vines to grow up it like a trellis."

"Boy, are you two nuts." Bill said, "Where are you going to get all that stuff? And what do you need a divider for anyway?"

"'Cause I want one, that's why," Jeanne answered him. "Okay, if you guys won't help us, that's okay. Geil and I'll figure out something."

"I just bet you will, too," Ed said and started smiling. "But just don't get Bill and me involved in any of your projects."

We were at a loss exactly how or where to begin. After considerable searching through stateside home furnishings magazines for a picture similar to what we wanted, we came up with an idea. I drew a picture to scale and explained to Kimiko what we wanted and asked her if she knew where we could get the frames.

"Hai, I know shoji store. I show you," Kimiko said and off we went in Jeanne's station wagon.

Using the picture and my diagrams, Jeanne's yardstick, and with a fair idea of what we wanted, Kimiko started talking to the owner of the store while Jeanne and I looked at the different styles and weights of frames. The conversation Kimiko was having seemed to be taking an unusually long time, so I asked her what the trouble was.

"He said dai jobu, he can do," she answered me, "but he sink more better if box rined with tin so water won't come out."

We hadn't thought of that!

"Ask him where we can get that done," Jeanne told her.

"Oh, he can do," replied Kimiko, "only it cost taku-san okane. Tin cost taku-san. He speak he do everysing, build, paint, make tin. Cost taku-san okane, maybe three thousand yen."

That was just under ten dollars, so Jeanne asked Kimiko to tell him to make it and find out when we could get it. After another long conversation, she told us, "He said come back two, three days."

Quite pleased with our deal, we could hardly wait for three days to pass to see what it was going to look like. Neither of us said a word about this to our husbands, thinking we'd surprise them. The third day we drove back to the shop and a pappa-san met us at the car door, bowing and shaking his head, "Ahh-ing" and "Ehh-ing" and sucking air in through his teeth. We hadn't the vaguest idea what he was trying to tell us.

We went back home for Kimiko. She told us he hadn't even started making the planter yet. I'm sure he thought our first trip was just a whim and we didn't really want such an expensive creation. However, to show his good intentions, he brought out some lumber and put his whole family to work immediately. Jeanne and I watched for a while, took a few pictures of the crude tools they were using, watched his son cut a piece of board he was standing on, sawing towards himself with a two-edged saw; and returned home a little disappointed.

After stopping at the store several times to check on the progress, the day arrived when the planter was finished. It looked awfully big. Had I measured wrong? We tried every conceivable way to load the planter in the station wagon without success. The framework was too big even after removing the planter box. It looked monstrous!

"What are we going to do with it now that it's done?" Jeanne asked, the doubts showing in her eyes.

"Let's go back and get Kimiko. We'll have to hold it on the outside of the car. She can sit in the very back, I'll sit in the middle, and you'll just have to drive with one hand, and hang on to it with the other."

"Do you think we can do it?"

"We'll have to. We don't dare ask the fellas to help us."

"Okay, you're right. But I sure hate to think of driving through this traffic with only one hand."

We got it back to Jeanne's without any major mishaps, although the wind pulled at the framework, and our arms felt paralyzed from the strain and cold.

Hiroko helped us move it inside where we assembled it and set it on top of two side-by-side bookcases (after rearranging all the living room furniture). Kimiko and Hiroko liked it. We had achieved our goal and had a perfect room divider—or would have, as soon as we got some soil and planted some greenery.

Intent on having it all finished before our husbands saw it urged us on in search of plants and good, clean soil. After a lengthy explanation of trying to describe the planter, the proprietor of a flower shop near Grant Heights showed us some plants that would grow well inside with little or no sunshine. Jeanne made her selection, and then she asked where we could get some soil.

"I want some good, clean dirt. I don't want any that's got honey buckets on it."

This message was translated to all the other clerks in the store and they giggled and tittered like school children.

"I have some. We no use honey buckets, only this," a clerk said, showing us some commercial fertilizer. "You have something to put it in?"

"We should have brought the planter," Jeanne said and started for the car. "Why didn't we think of that?"

"I don't want to take that planter all apart," I said. "Can't we use buckets or something? I've got one bucket and some old coffee cans. Don't you have something we can haul dirt in, Jeanne? I don't know how much it will take, but I would guess it'll take a lot of dirt."

The planter box was approximately seventy-two inches by nine inches by eight inches. Collecting all the available scrub buckets, coffee cans, sand pails, cardboard boxes we could find at both houses, we returned for the dirt.Jeanne planted the greenery, artistically arranging the vines on the latticework.

That evening, when I had Bill go over to see the room divider, he and Ed finally admitted it wasn't a bad idea and that it did improve the looks of the room. Jeanne and I were smugly pleased with ourselves. This project, and other ordinarily trifling tasks, had involved a lot of work, but they'd been a challenge to our ingenuity; the rewards were gratifying; and, besides being kept busy, we were getting a first-hand education of Japan.

31

I stayed home one day to do some sewing as I needed to get some mending done and some new spring clothes made. I was just getting into the swing of sewing and feeling I could get a lot accomplished when the most horrible, sickening odor came through the open window and moved on through the whole house. The rank odor was so intense I was positive it couldn't be coming from honey buckets down on the street, so I started a search for its origin. When I got to the front door I met Kimiko coming in.

"Oku-san, what I do now? I hang crlean clothes up to dry and now Pappa-san, he put taku-san honey bucket all over ground. Crlothes no smell so good now, I sink."

I went out to see where Pappa-san was pouring the night soil. To my utter amazement, the farmer who lived back of us was pouring it on his field, about two feet from the back of our house. I could understand Kimiko's concern about the clothes. The wind was blowing off the field and the air outside was more abominable than it had been inside. What could we do? The clothes had just been washed and would have to dry, regardless of how they smelled, or they'd mildew.

The scene I had just witnessed presented a new concern for me. The well that pumped water for the five houses was located at the back of our house. It was only a shallow well, and the water wasn't purified in any way. All this time we'd just been boiling the water for drinking! Now, I wasn't so sure that was good enough. Rather than take any more chances, I decided to pick up chlorinated water from Jeanne's house for drinking and cooking. Of course, we would still have to use this water for bathing and laundry, which didn't particularly appeal to me either right then.

Oh well! C'est la vie, c'est la guerre, I thought. Just one more of the insurmountable problems of living in a foreign country.

32

It was about time for the cherry blossoms to start blooming, and I'd always heard how beautiful they were and wanted to see them. Bill drove us to Meiji Park in downtown Tokyo, but because of the late arrival of spring, the trees were only partially blossomed out. We did take a few pictures of the blossoms amidst all of the other well cared for and carefully pruned trees.

When we noticed a Japanese family taking pictures, too, we moved out of the way so they could get an unobstructed view of the trees. But they waved and motioned to us, and to our surprise they wanted pictures of us! We posed as a family for them, and it made me very self-conscious, realizing that we were as different to them as they were to us. The shoe was on the other foot now. This taught me to be more considerate in my picture taking, and I either asked permission or at least tried to appear as a friend and not as an oddity seeker.

The cherry trees, in defiance of the late, cold spring, finally burst into full bloom. The blossoms ranged in colors from pure white, pale pink, deep pink, lavender and some pale green. The flowers blooming on trees bare of any leaves looked like large wads of cotton candy stuck on the branches.

I never did understand how there could be so many cherry blossoms but never any cherries.

On a day the children didn't have school, Jeanne and I planned a trip to a park. Tokoshima Park was only a short distance back of Grant Heights and she knew how to drive there. However, not sure we could find our way around in the park, we asked Kimiko and Hiroko to go with us. It was about a twenty-minute drive over dirt roads, congested with busses loaded with Japanese children. The sun had been out when we left, but by the time we reached the park it had disappeared, which was par for the course for us.

The natural stream, lined on either side by cherry trees heavy laden with buds and blossoms bending out over the stream, emanated a beauty of Nature for which I, at least, was unprepared. I would have enjoyed roaming around longer enjoying the scenery and flowers, the little bridges and rock formations. But the children were restlessly in search of more exciting things.

Bordering this garden spot we found all kinds of rides similar to those at our carnivals and fairs, but the designs of the cars or cabs were different. A few of the unique ones: A merry-go-round that had big, pink wooden elephants, and instead of the children straddling them, the seats were sunk into the backs; a small train for children with each car in the shape of a different animal or bird; a Shetland pony hitched to a little old-fashioned surrey with fringe on top; an airplane ride (looking like one of our first Army trainers); and a huge world, constructed out of what appeared to be heavy steel wire forming the longitude and latitude lines of the earth, revolved on an angle as the earth turns on its axis, with a narrow platform upon which the participants stood encircled the inside of this huge globe at the equator line. This gigantic ride, where the passengers were so high they appeared to be small, dark shadows, looked dangerous even for adults and, thank goodness, it didn't appeal to any of the children.

One of the most thrilling rides to watch (none of us were brave enough to try it) was a boat that came down a steep ramp and hit the water with a terrific force and a huge splash. Using this impact for thrust, a Japanese boy-san standing on the front of the boat, with perfect coordination and superb athletic form, would leap into the air doing flips, somersaults, or other acrobatic antics, and never once missed landing on the front end of the boat, nor lost his balance, nor upset the boat. Other boy-sans wading in the lake would grab the boat as it slowed down and guide it over to the side to unload the damp passengers and reload it with more brave souls.

The children's rides cost us only ten and twenty yen (about three to six cents) a ride, so the children enjoyed a full afternoon's fun at very little cost. Bonnie and Jeff particularly let themselves go, squealing and yelling with delight during the rides—quite the opposite of the Japanese children's reactions, who, like their parents, showed no emotion whatsoever as to whether they liked or disliked any of the rides.

In addition to the many rides, the park provided picnic grounds where groups of Japanese were sitting on benches or on the ground eating their dried fish and rice and drinking sake; restaurants; boating in the river (mostly young couples with the girls doing the rowing); a little fishing pool stocked with goldfish (if you caught one, it was put in a soft drink bottle to take home); and a very small zoo with one small, moth-eaten bear, a pair of peacocks, some birds and a few small animals that I didn't recognize and I couldn't read the signs. Although we could have managed quite well in the park without the maids, they enjoyed the day's outing every bit as much as we did.

33

Confident of being on our own, Jeanne and I caught an early morning bus to spend a day in the very heart of downtown Tokyo. Dressed in suits, hats and white gloves—proper city clothing—we made good connections at all of the transfer points, taking in a tour of the Tokyo PX along the way.

At the end of the bus line in the center of town, we started walking, exploring Matusuya Department Store on the Ginza (the most famous street in Tokyo), and several other of the larger department stores. Employees lined up just inside the entrances of these stores, bowed low as we entered, saying, "Ohayo gozaimasu" (good morning) or "Konnichi-wa" (good day) and "Domo arigato " (thank you very much) as we left.

Shortly after our arrival on any floor, we were greeted by an English-speaking clerk who offered her assistance. This was all very impressive, and we felt guilty just "window shopping" so we purchased some toys for the children.

We decided on the Civilian Service Club for lunch, as neither of us particularly cared for Japanese food, and we didn't know how to pick a good restaurant. Returning to the bus terminal, we checked all the incoming and outgoing GI busses for some time but never could figure out which one went by the club.

While we stood there a little Japanese shoe-shine boy pestered us with questions in English about where we wanted to go, what bus we wanted, and insisted he could get us a cab or bus to anywhere we wanted to go. We tried to ignore him, figuring he would want a sizable tip for getting us a cabby who would probably charge us double fare. But the little shoc-shine boy just wouldn't give up.

Nonplussed, we tossed our heads in a sophisticated manner and strode across the street like seasoned world travelers and hailed a little cab. Most of the cabs were quite small, about the size of Volkswagens (nicknamed "Ten-Yen Cabs" by the Americans).

Jeanne told the driver the name of the club and the cabbie answered, "Hai." He took off like a shot out of a cannon, throwing us roughly against the back and knocking our hats off. Right then the clouds burst open releasing a downpour which the windshield wipers couldn't keep up with. The impaired visibility increased the everyday traffic hazards of cabs and cars weaving in and out without signals, plus the onslaught of trotting jay-walkers with their black umbrellas pulled down low around their shoulders. Dropping our heads in our hands, we covered our eyes, convinced our cab driver must be an ex-kamikaze pilot who was taking us with him on his suicidal drive.

The civilian club wasn't too far from the bus terminal, and at that speed we should have already arrived. Jeanne peeked through her fingers to see where we were. Then she rubbed the steam off of the window and peered out but still couldn't see a familiar landmark in any direction.

"My gosh, where are we?" she said and tapped the driver on the shoulder. "You are taking us to the civilian club, aren't you?"

"Hai," he said and kept right on going.

"Do you suppose he doesn't understand English?" I said, my voice quivering. "Or is he just taking us the long way to run up his meter?"

"I don't know, but we gotta do something fast. His driving is scaring me to death." She started pounding on his back, nearly shouting, "Chotto matte, we want to go to civilian club. You understand? Club, for chop-chop—a place to eat."

He slammed on his brakes, throwing us against the front seat. He looked around at us, giving us a toothpaste commercial grin, and hissed, "Ah-so."

Almost simultaneously he had the car in gear, burning rubber as he made skidding U-turn to the left, bounced up over the curb, down the sidewalk, and shot across the oncoming lane of traffic with brakes squealing all around us. Thank goodness the back seat was small, or we'd have ended up on the floor instead of being knocked together.

Still not sure that he'd understood Jeanne, we kept looking for a familiar sign, all to no avail. Then, around a corner, up a hill, a quick slam on the brakes and he was out of the cab and had the door open for us (before we had a chance to pull our skirts down over our knees), bowing low and smiling. He'd driven us to the commissary at one of the dependent housing areas in the Tokyo area, not the club.

I was ready to get out and forget the cabbie, but Jeanne recognized the place and knew how to get to the club from the commissary.

"How many words of Japanese do you know, Geil?"

"Not very many, why?"

"I'm going to try to direct him to the Club. I'm sure he doesn't understand English—Massugu," she told him.

"Migi means right," I added hopefully.

"Oh, that's right. But what's left?"

"Let's see, massuga means straight ahead; migi means right," I said hoping the association of words would help me remember. "Golly, Jeanne, I just can't think of it."

By using only these two words and pointing, Jeanne directed the cabbie to our destination. We gladly paid him for the long ride, just thankful we had arrived in one piece, safe and sound, even though our nylons and skirts were half twisted around our body and our hats sitting at a rakish angle.

That evening we related our adventure to our husbands. They laughed hilariously and said we should've listened to the little shoe-shine boy. They told us he would have directed us to the right GI bus or gotten us a cab at a reasonable charge, with no extra ride or extra fare, and that he was truly a friend-in-need to Americans.

We had learned another lesson the hard way.

34

"Oku-san, come quick, dozo," Kimiko called.

"What is it?" I asked, going into the kitchen.

"Look," pointing to the shelves.

"What's causing the bottles to jiggle? Look, everything's moving."

"Hai, taku-san big earthquake, I sink," she said and hurried towards the door. "More better we go outside."

A real live earthquake—and I was actually experiencing one! The hypnotic swaying of articles and pendulum swinging of the two hanging wall planters held me more spellbound than afraid. The earth's shaking was much like the jarring caused by large trucks as they rumbled by on the highway, except the trucks didn't cause things to jiggle and sway.

When Bonnie got home from school that afternoon she said the ceiling lights in their schoolroom swayed so hard, cracking one whole wall, the teacher was afraid the lights would fall. All of the children had been evacuated from the building to the safety of the outdoors where nothing could fall on them.

Kimiko told us that several years ago Tokyo had had such a severe earthquake that the ground shook so hard people couldn't walk, but had to literally crawl along the ground.

That evening Bill described his experience during the earthquake. His office was several stories high and the higher up the more severe the shaking. Karaki-san, the interpreter in MAAG-J, had explained to Bill that the really damaging earthquakes usually follow a certain pattern in fairly close sequence. The first, the earth shakes back and forth. If a second quake follows within a few minutes with the earth rolling in the opposite direction, it is best to get out of any building, because if a third one occurs, it's almost certain to be a shaking and rolling at the same time, a combination which is almost impossible for any building to withstand.

Knowing what to expect and what to do dispelled my newfound fears; nevertheless, I maintained a great respect for quakes and I didn't doubt the havoc they could wreak. None of the many little ones I felt after that particularly upset me, but I certainly had a better understanding of why there were no skyscrapers in Japan.

35

Bonnie's after-school activities were limited and I enrolled her in a dancing class at Narimasu School. She'd taken dancing lessons since she was five and was more advanced than most of the other children. The teacher used her as a student teacher and offered to give her private lessons in her home at Pershing Heights. Bill drove us there the first couple of times, and then Bonnie and I became regular commuters on the bus.

Pershing Heights was immaculately clean and beautiful. The gleaming white cement buildings were erected on a high bluff. A wide, curving, crushed rock driveway led up to the main building, in front of which was a concrete parade ground and three tall flagpoles, from which the United States flag and the United Nations flag were flown.

This was now the United Nations Far Eastern Command Headquarters, but had been General McArthur's headquarters during the United States' occupation of Japan. The large, two-story barracks buildings had been remodeled into apartments. The grounds were beautifully landscaped with large boulders, odd-shaped trees that had been carefully pruned and trained to grow in particular shapes, and flowering bushes, all of which were artistically united by lawn and gravel. From the edge of the cliff we could look out over the rooftops of the buildings below, the houses jammed up to each other with only small yards, laced together with narrow roads. The grounds underneath the main building contained emergency passageways for evacuation from the buildings.

Military and civilian dignitaries of other countries conducted their business with the UNFEC at this site, and during their presence the flag of their country was flown from the third flagpole. We always checked to see what country was represented on the days we were there. It was a very impressive place and made me more aware of the world situation and of the manner in which it was being handled.

36

There had been several attempted burglaries of our American neighbors, and one night the people living right next to us were robbed while they slept. The robber had used glass cutters to cut out their kitchen window, crawled through and apparently used some sort of chloroform or something else to induce them to a deeper sleep so he had plenty of time to gather up all the blankets, sheets, money and ID cards without being interrupted.

A bevy of policemen arrived to investigate and take fingerprints (they even identified Bill's, as he had inadvertently leaned on the sill looking through the window), and were quite thorough in their checking the clues and getting a list of stolen items. This robbery completely unnerved the neighboring Americans. During the next few days our landlord had Pappasan put strong, wooden bars over all our windows for protection against a repeat performance, which made us feel like we were living in a jail.

Kimiko learned from one of the investigating policemen that we should go to our neighborhood police station and register so they would have the authority to protect us. Also, we could tell them whenever we were to be gone for more than a day and they would keep a close watch on our house. This made good sense to me, not only because of the recent robbery, but because Bill's work oftentimes took him on long, overnight trips, and we were left alone. (Kimiko always spent the night with us when Bill was away.)

I wasted no time in going to the police station, which was about a block from our house. Kimiko told the policeman who

I was and what I wanted. He couldn't speak a word of English, but was friendly and very courteous, bowing several times. A long form covered with Japanese printing had to be filled out. He would read a question to Kimiko, who translated it into English for me. I would answer her, and she translated it into Japanese for him. Then he laboriously wrote the answer down in that fabulous Japanese printing. This manner of questioning and answering was a very slow process and took a long time.

During the interrogation, I looked around in this little police station. Such a lived-in look this little, one-room building had. Handcuffs, billy clubs, clean uniforms and other police equipment were hanging on nails driven into the walls. A single light bulb dangled on a cord from the ceiling over a small wooden desk which was cluttered with printed forms, a telephone, stacked tea cups, rice bowls and chopsticks. The small hibachi was keeping a teapot warm. The place looked more like a home than a station house where four or more policemen took turns of being on duty.

After our extensive interview, we were ready to leave. The friendly policeman, grinning broadly, bowed low several times, thanked me and assured me (according to Kimiko) he would keep close watch of our place. Not only had I found a good protector, but I had also made a new friend.

37

On a Saturday afternoon when the sun was shining brightly, Bill, Bonnie and I decided on a sight-seeing tour. Driving through one of the larger cemeteries, we became so intrigued we finally parked the car and toured on foot.

Aoyama Bochi, right in the heart of Tokyo, had apparently been there for many, many years. Each of the small burial lots, surrounded by a low cement or stone wall, contained one tombstone. The tombstones ran the full gamut of sizes and shapes—some quite large and completely covered with Japanese writing. (We discovered later that these gave the complete history of the family buried there.) Some were so old the weathered, moss-covered stones were almost black; and new ones were beautifully sculptured in ultra-modern designs. Some lots had only wooden sticks in place of the tombstones because they were either new graves or the family was too poor to afford a stone.

Whether simple or ornate, all lots contained a standard set of equipment consisting of cement outdoor lantern (used for burning candles so that the spirits could find their way back from their various excursions), a built-in incense burner and a permanently installed vase or urn for fresh flowers. The grounds were beautifully landscaped with large trees and flowering shrubs, and the whole area had the appearance of a park instead of a cemetery. It was peaceful and serene, rather than spooky.

Discussing this excursion with Kimiko, she furnished me with more information. Birthdays, as such, are never celebrated in Japan; however, the date of a person's death is almost always remembered. On such an anniversary it is customary to burn incense at the cemetery and at home; prepare the favorite foods of the deceased, a bowl of which is placed on the tokonoma, or home altar, so the spirit won't go hungry; and often the friends of the departed one are invited in for this memorial which more nearly resembles our birthday parties.

The wooden slats we had observed at the bochi, stuck in around the tombstones, were proof that members of the family had visited the cemetery on the day set aside for such visits. (Higan or Equinoctial, in March and September). The remaining head of the household, followed by the rest of the family, make this annual visit to the cemetery at which time the tombstone and other stone decorations are scrubbed clean, fresh flowers arranged, incense burned, prayers offered, and food left at the bochi for the spirits.

Kimiko further explained that most Japanese, except for

the Christians, are still cremated. When a member of the family dies, unless they are of the very wealthy class, the body is prepared by the mother or oldest daughter of the family. After the body has been washed and oiled (or whatever preparation they use), it is clothed in his or her best kimono, white tabis (ankle-length socks with a split toe so getas or zoris can be worn), and a cane or walking stick for the long journey in the hereafter is placed beside the body. The body is picked up in a hearse (or "sayonara wagon," as the Americans nick-named them), the sides of carved wood topped with a tiled roof, with the more expensive hearses trimmed in gold. The hearse delivers the body to the crematory, or what Kimiko called the "fire house."

The wealth of the family determines the size and fanciness or plainness of the room furnished. As soon as all the flesh is burned and nothing left except the bones, the head of the family, or oldest son, using fire-proof, over-sized chopsticks, picks the bones from the ashes, passes them down the line to each member of the family and the last person drops them into an urn. When all the bones are placed in the urn, it is returned to the home where it is kept for a week before taken to the bochi.

At the cemetery, the bones are deposited in the tombstone or large receptacle for that purpose by means of a secret sliding door. Consequently, a whole family's bones can be deposited in a rather small space.

I was never able to distinguish the basic difference between the religions of Buddhism and Shinto. Kimiko was a Buddhist. She said her husband was a Christian. But, she said, "He no do nussing. I be Christian, I no do nussing, too. More better I stay Buddhist."

I did learn that the Buddhists believe in reincarnation. Kimiko was very kind to all animals because she didn't want to be kicked by people when she came back as a dog or cat.

The Shinto had various idols they worshipped and offered sacrifices; for example, when a baby was seriously ill, a piece of that baby's clothing was placed on a certain statue and left to rot away. These shrines or temples with idols were scattered all over the city. In the farmlands, many farmers had their own statues.

This all seemed rather gruesome, but from our conversations I realized how the Japanese could commit hari-kari and why there were so many kamikaze pilots during the War. They were not afraid of death but accepted it as a way of life.

38

As Jeanne was doing more and more sewing, she discovered she had no place to keep her ever-growing number of spools of thread. She liked the thread box I'd brought from the States and wanted one like it. The Japanese are artists at copying anything, but it would be too complicated to try to explain the thread box. So we carried mine a couple of blocks down the street to a bamboo store.

The thread box, about twenty inches by twenty-four inches, has little legs with handles on top and it opens like a book standing up on end. Opened, the left side has nine little shelves with little spindles to hold twelve spools of thread to a shelf, and the right side has six shelves, spaced farther apart, to hold the larger spools of thread, and a compartment at the top for scissors, tape, etc.

The little carpenter "ah-soed" as he checked it over, measured it and drew a picture of it in a little notebook, making notes about size, etc. We had Kimiko with us as our interpreter, and she told us it would be ready in about a week. Sure enough, a week later Jeanne got her duplicate of my thread box. Two or three weeks later, several copies of my thread box had been added to his line of merchandise.

Kimiko was, indeed, a jewel. Like a diamond in the rough—not highly polished, but many sided. She was a maid, interpreter, protector, adviser, companion and friend all rolled into one. Plus she had her whimsical humor.

She had her set routine for doing certain jobs each day. When the Leys stopped by one afternoon she was just cleaning the living room, as I'd delayed her by using her on some errand that morning. Not wanting to further disrupt her routine and knowing that Jeanne would understand, I permitted Kimiko to continue cleaning. She manipulated the vacuum around everyone's feet until she came to Jeanne.

"Mrs. Ray, you rift feet, dozo?"

Raising her feet so Kimiko could vacuum under them, Jeanne went on talking not paying any attention to her.

"Sukoshi higher, dozo."

Jeanne lifted her feet a little higher.

"Mo sukoshi, dozo."

"Kimiko, what are you trying to do?" Jeanne asked, grabbing her knees to hold her legs up. "Are you trying to see if I can get my feet above my head?"

"Hai, I sink so. I sink serlgeant can see more better then," she said, placing her hand over her mouth to control her tittering.

"What's that, Kimiko?" Bill asked, his attention diverted from Ed. "So I can see what more better?"

"Gol dang you, Kimiko," Jeanne said, faking indignation as she slammed her feet back down on the floor and with exaggerated motions pulled her skirt down over her knees. "Who put you up to that?—Bill, are you the guilty one?"

Throwing his hands up in mock surrender, "I didn't do it. I didn't see a thing—I was just sitting here talking to the major."

"Did I miss out on something?" Ed asked. "Kimiko, what are you up to now?"

"Serlgeant no do. I do. I sink I sukoshi not so nice girl."

And momentarily stripped of her protective stoic upbringing, Kimiko's giggling gushed forth uncontrollably.

It was a game in which we all participated with nonsensical palaver and over-action, each trying to outdo the other.

This tomfoolery was usually between the four of us with Kimiko playing the part of the participating audience. This time, having turned the trick on us, we enjoyed the spoof as much as she.

39

Because of the riotous parades of the Communists, May 1 was declared a holiday from work and school for all Americans, who were warned to stay in their homes, on base or in government housing areas as a precautionary measure to avoid any riots or unfortunate incidents that might provoke a serious situation. The Leys, having witnessed the past May Day celebration when American cars had been tipped over and school busses stopped, were kind enough to ask us and another military family, also living in private rental, to spend the entire day with them. Betty and I fixed food and we three families spent an enjoyable day trying to eat all the food, playing euchre and chatting. The six children had a wonderfully full day of play.

Most of the merry-makers had congregated in downtown Tokyo, where Japanese policemen were out in full force to control any trouble that might arise. Fortunately, the rainy day not only drenched the participants but also dampened their spirits so no major catastrophes developed.

Kai-Nabori, or Boys' Day, is celebrated on May 5 and the prior week large red and white paper fish and colored streamers strung up on tall poles began appearing at almost every house. Ropes were used to hoist them to their high position on a plain bamboo pole or on one topped with a very ornate gold-plated or brass decoration that would spin in the breeze.

These paper fish indicated a son in the family. Some homes

displayed several fish, one for each son, in graduated sizes with the largest at the top.

Fashioned out of paper and silk, varying in size from three feet to fifteen feet long and possibly eighteen inches in diameter, the ends were open so the least little breeze would billow them out and give the illusion of fish swimming (the streamers represented a waterfall). Symbolizing a carp, this one hundred twenty-five year old custom of flying fish signified strength, determination, ambition, and self-discipline. All the traits that anyone could desire endowed in their sons.

Although Boy's Day was no longer a national holiday in Japan, it was a school holiday and some sections had big parades with fancy floats. The boys' collections, consisting of old warrior dolls in full battle dress, historical princes and heroes, miniature armor, and carved animals (mostly horses), were exhibited and revered as the girls' dolls, and handed down from son to son for many generations.

Bonnie and I attended the showing at Narimasu School, grateful for the opportunity of observing and learning, but it wasn't quite as interesting to us as the girls' collections.

40

Apparently our acquisition of a canary and gold fish convinced Pappa-san that we were pet lovers and one day he had a present-o for Bonnie—three of the biggest tadpoles I'd ever seen. Pappa-san had caught them himself and described with his hands that they would grow into frogs about the size of big dinner plates, which I could well believe. The tadpoles were three to four inches long and fat as butter balls.

Temporarily depositing them in the bathtub partially filled with water, I went down to the corner where a saleslady parked her pushcart full of pots and pans and bought a big, round, brass Japanese dishpan.

Bonnie and Kimiko cared for the tadpoles, and we all interestingly watched their growth. These tadpoles were really lively, swimming around and around in the dishpan, sometimes gaining so much momentum they would fly right out of the pan. I didn't like touching the slimy, wiggly things, so Bonnie and Kimiko kept close tab on them, retrieving any "flyer" and putting him back in the pan.

For some reason I'd always believed the tails of tadpoles dropped off; but instead, the tails receded and grew shorter as the legs emerged and grew longer. When the tadpoles finally developed into small frogs and able to hop around, it was impossible to keep them in the dishpan. Not wanting them hopping all over the house, we moved the pan and frogs into the bathroom where they had full run of the large, tiled room as well as the pan of water. The door was kept closed, not only because it opened off of the living room, but mainly to keep the frogs confined.

They grew rapidly and had such long legs and bulgy eyes that I dreaded going into the bathroom with these little creatures hopping all around. In the hope of scaring them into hiding under the tub, I always pounded on the door before entering. I'll never forget the night I went in after knocking. I didn't see them anywhere. As I reached to turn on the water in the lavatory, this bulgy-eyed little character was staring up at me from the basin as if he owned the place and I shouldn't disturb him. I got his message and left in a big hurry, without washing my hands, figuring he could get out of the lavatory the same way he got in. I was ready to throw them all out right then and there, but Bill and Bonnie talked me out of it.

During the next few weeks one by one they started disappearing. We weren't sure what happened, but they liked the cool dampness under the tub and we figured they were probably washed down the drain when water ran out of the tub. Admittedly, I missed them when they were gone. They were interesting, but I don't recommend them for pets.

41

The rainy season was finally over, followed by lovely sunny days. Jeanne wanted her backyard fenced in so she could leave the children's toys outside and they could have a little privacy. She asked our pappa-san if he would build a fence for her and if he knew where she could buy some bamboo cheap, knowing the Japanese could buy local items much cheaper than Americans. Pappa-san couldn't understand what she wanted, so we relied again on Kimiko.

"Pappa-san say he do," she told us, "and he know ichi-ban bamboo man. He speak more better if Oku-san drive us there."

The four of us piled into Jeanne's station wagon and started on our way to the ichi-ban bamboo man's home via directions from Pappa-san translated by Kimiko. After a short distance she directed Jeanne to turn off on a very narrow dirt road lined with little shabby houses, smaller and more deteriorated than most we'd seen. On arrival in this little neighborhood, as though our coming had been heralded, mamma-sans, pappa-sans, kodomos (children), grandmas, grandpas, dogs, cats, chickens, etc., appeared en masse out of nowhere, surrounding the car and impairing our progress. Momentarily, we weren't sure whether we were being mobbed or welcomed, and then Kimiko told us we were parked in front of Pappa-san's house and he wanted to show us something.

Bracing ourselves for the onslaught of inquisitiveness, we all four climbed out of the car and followed Pappa-san. Kimiko, pointing to a woman squatted on the ground at the side of a house scrubbing clothes in a pan, whispered she was Pappa-san's Oku-san. With an uncertain smile and slight nod, she acknowledged our presence and continued with her washing. Pappa-san ignored her completely.

Sliding open the outer door of his little house, he proudly showed us his many little homemade wooden cages containing canaries. With his usual guttural sounds, he went into great detail explaining and pointing out each individual cage—some were singers, some building nests, a mamma bird was sitting on her nest of eggs, some had newly hatched babies being fed by the parent birds, and some older ones that hadn't fledged yet were in another cage, one of which Pappa-san gently picked up and demonstrated how he fed them a prepared mash with a very small paddle. He also showed us the little rice paper sliding windows he'd made to fit on the cages to keep the birds atsui, or warm.

I'd learned to "bend with the bamboo" and not fight a situation or try to hurry someone along, so we temporarily forgot our primary reason for being there and enjoyed the discourse on the breeding and raising of canaries.

While Kimiko and Pappa-san were talking with each other and Jeanne's car was being scrutinized inch by inch, inside and out by the neighbors, I sneaked glances at our varied spectators. Most were dressed in their native work clothes. I was particularly fascinated by a little, old, wrinkled gentleman standing towards the rear of the crowd. He stood only a little over four feet tall; his snow white beard, about one-half inch long, was sparsely scattered over his face and stuck straight out like the quills on a porcupine. He was peering over the top of a pair of small, round silver-edged spectacles, perched quite low on his flat nose. He was dressed in a long, brown kimono (worn by men around the house or on their trip to and from the bathhouse), his dingy long underwear peeking out at his wrists and ankles, and a pair of worn getas were on his gnarled bare feet. He was so unique and adorable, I was trying to figure out how I could get a picture of him when Kimiko pointed to him saying he was the ichi-bon bamboo man we were looking for.

Pappa-san and our picturesque little character, whom Kimiko said we should call Oji-san (grandfather or old man), began a long, gesticulatory conversation and the crowd began dispersing. During this conversation, both men would look at us and every now and then Oji-san would smile and bow low to us. Curiosity got the better of me and I asked Kimiko what they were talking about. She said it was just friendly neighborhood talk, then an explanation of who we were, and finally our purpose for being there.

To our delight, Oji-san said he knew where we could get good bamboo and would direct us there. He got right into Jeanne's car, not even waiting for us to ask him or even bothering to change his clothes. This was a little embarrassing, as I wasn't in the habit of going shopping with a man dressed in his underwear and a bathrobe. No one else was upset about it, so I supposed it was customary, and we all got in the car and Oji-san directed us on to the bamboo store.

Oji-san, Pappa-san and the three men at the store repeated the long ritual of bowing, the friendly little chatter and at long last why we were there, after which Kimiko explained to them what Jeanne wanted. She translated for us that the men had asked if she were the honsho, or boss. (Japanese women were seldom allowed to have any authority.) She thought it "more better" if we drew a picture.

Returning to the men with a hastily sketched picture indicating approximate measurements, Kimiko became involved in a further discussion with the men, trying to explain our measurements on Jeanne's yardstick.

To while away the time I took a few pictures, and when Oji-san realized I had a camera, he had Kimiko ask me to take a picture of him. This was just what I'd wanted! (Later, I had a colored print made for him which pleased him ever so much.)

Their conversation continued on endlessly, long enough for all four men, except Pappa-san, at different times to just turn their backs and urinate. Leaning over and wiping her legs off with some Kleenex, Jeanne uttered disgustedly, "Gosh darn it. You'd think he could have at least gone over by the bushes to let it fly instead of standing right here and splattering me."

"Oji-san speak more better build fence maybe three feet high, not four feet. Bamboo come six feet, other two feet no good. Make fence cost taku-san okane," Kimiko finally reported.

"Oh, good heavens, what'll we do?" Jeanne asked me. "The housing authority specified any fence built had to be four feet high. Others have fences. Where do you suppose they got the right length bamboo?"

"Beats me. But what do they mean that bamboo comes in only six feet lengths? Look at all these stacks of bamboo," I answered, pointing around us to the big supply of bamboo poles standing up on end. "I don't see any that short. Looks like they're anywhere from ten feet to twenty or thirty feet long."

I asked Kimiko about this, but she could give me no logical explanation, nor could she get one from any of the men. Each of them drew a picture of the way he thought the fence should be like—one wanted to build it so it would have small window-like openings at varying heights scattered all through the fence; another suggested using three foot lengths of bamboo, building the fence up twelve inches off the ground; and still another suggested an open trellis-like fence.

Jeanne finally told them she wanted a solid bamboo fence, four feet high. But if they couldn't furnish four foot lengths, then they would have to use the three foot lengths, but they were not to leave more than three or four inches between the bottom of the fence and the ground (hoping the housing authorities wouldn't come measure the fence).

Once the decision had been made it didn't take long for them to figure out how much bamboo, how many corner poles, and how much horse hair, used to tie the bamboo together, was needed; and they started loading the supplies on a little three-wheeled truck. When Jeanne had left home that morning, it had been her intention to just get an estimate of how much a fence would cost; but there they were with the truck loaded, ready to follow us to her home.

Another lesson had been learned (which was confirmed later): To always be sure of exactly what we wanted when we went for anything. The Japanese are very reticent about making a decision when asked for advice, and would much prefer it to be done by someone "above" them.

Once all the material was unloaded at Jeanne's house, it wasn't too many days until Pappa-san and Oji-san dressed in his knickers, old work coat and a white hat resembling a painter's cap, had completed the fence.

This enclosure became the source of many hours' pleasure not only for the children, who particularly enjoyed their little plastic swimming pool, but also for us. Many picnics, barbecues and just lazy afternoons and weekends of relaxing in the sun were spent there.

42

Mr. Nokomura, our landlord, stopped by the house one day and asked Kimiko how he might get in touch with the Leys. Upon learning they lived on Grant Heights, he very apologetically asked her if I would mind driving him there, as he wasn't allowed on the housing area unless accompanied by an American. He seemed so intent on seeing the Leys, and since our car was sitting in the parking lot, I didn't have the heart to turn him down.

Bill had joined a car pool, leaving the car home four days of the week in case I would ever need transportation, but I had never been brave enough to try driving. It was only about six blocks to Jeanne's, most of which was in the housing area. Surely, I could get the car there and back. So, unbeknown to Mr. Nokomura that this was my first driving in Japan, we started off. Very cautiously I backed out on N Avenue, and then proceeded forward, edging into the right, inside lane of the left side of the road, and made the right turn into Grant Heights.

It didn't seem very sociable to sit there and not say anything, so I nervously carried on a one-sided conversation, knowing he couldn't understand a word I said. There was no traffic on Grant Heights, I was getting along fine and I wondered why I'd been so afraid of driving. Confidently, I turned the next corner. Glancing at Mr. Nokomura, I saw his "pasted-on" smile had disappeared, his head was rigid, eyes staring straight ahead, his hands gripping the seat, and his feet shoved up against the floorboards. What was scaring him so? I was driving very carefully and slowly—and then I understood his fright.

A car was coming towards us in my lane of traffic! In a split second I had to decide. Was I in the right lane, or was the right lane in the left lane? No, I was wrong. I was in the right lane and the right lane was the wrong lane, and the left lane was the right lane. I spun the steering wheel to the left, barely in time to avoid a head-on collision!

Mr. Nokomura took care of his business with Jeanne while I sat down and had a cigarette. The trip home was uneventful. Not wanting to upset Mr. Nokumura any more than I had, I forgot about talking and concentrated on my driving, remembering to stay in the left lane, keeping a watchful eye on traffic. Having successfully accomplished the first test of my driving skill (thanks to Mr. Nokomura), each day I practiced driving by going to the commissary for groceries or to the gas station for drinking water or just over to see Jeanne until it felt familiar driving in the left lane.

43

The beauty shop at Grant Heights was always filled with appointments so far in advance Jeanne and I hesitated making an appointment. We enjoyed being free to do things on the spur of the moment. A Japanese beauty shop near our house had attracted us with its sign, "Parmanent Shop." So once again we braved the unknown to try our luck.

Upon entering the entryway, we found straw slippers fashioned like bedroom mules stuck in little cubby holes for the customers' use. After slipping our shoes off and slipping into the mules, we parted the curtains and stepped up into the beauty shop. Two girl operators met us, bowed low and motioned us to a settee, handing us several Japanese magazines full of pictures of various hair styles.

Browsing through the magazines until we found a style similar to what we each wanted, and using hand motions, we conveyed the message we wanted our hair cut like the one in the picture. A little leery about how our haircuts would turn out, Jeanne and I exchanged a giddy banter about how our hair would probably be cut like a Japanese school girl's, sort of a Buster Brown, or something completely different than what we wanted. The beauty operators were giggling and chattering away in Japanese as they cut our hair.

As it turned out, we were quite pleased with our haircuts and even more so when we learned a haircut cost only twenty-five cents in American money. We became regular customers at the Parmanent Shop in the weeks ahead, and finally let the girls give us a permanent. A few days later I noticed an article in one of the local newspapers that many Japanese women were losing their hair and going bald as a result of a certain permanent waving lotion. This news really upset me and, after telling Jeanne about it, we kept close watch of each other's head to see if we were going bald. Nothing like that happened, thank goodness, but it's a wonder we didn't lose all our hair just from the worry. The next time we needed a permanent we used one of our ration stamps, bought a home permanent kit at the PX and let the girls use that.

The beauty operators were quite adept at fixing our hair the way we liked it, and would often throw in a manicure. They'd even comb our hair when we just stopped in to make an appointment. We'd wash our hair at my place and then, with towels wrapped around our heads, go dashing down the street to the shop taking our own combs and brushes. During cold weather we'd sit with our winter coats on, shivering from the cold air whistling in around us. But for only twenty-five cents a trip, we didn't mind these little inconveniences.

On one visit I was aghast at seeing one of the girls shaving a Japanese lady's face with a straight-edged razor as an American man is shaved in a barber shop. Not believing my eyes, I could hardly wait to get back to ask Kimiko about it. She said yes, many Japanese women shave, especially if they wear makeup, otherwise the makeup wouldn't look nice and smooth if applied over the "peach fuzz" hair on women's faces. This I'd never heard of, but then I'd never become so concerned about my makeup that I'd ever take up shaving.

44

The tin sink in our house had rusted until it was impossible to clean. Bill asked our landlord about a new one, but apparently he thought it cost too much money. A sink and benjo store was just up the street from our house, so I took Kimiko and Pappa-san there one afternoon to find out how much a new sink would cost, and to be sure I would get the right size.

After about an hour of haggling over the price, finding one of the right size and color combination, and one which had the drain hole in the correct corner for our plumbing system, the purchase was made, the sink loaded on a bicycle and delivered to our house.

The new sink cost two thousand yen (a little more than five dollars) and it was worth every penny to have a decent tile sink that would not only look better but would be so much easier to keep clean. Pappa-san installed it—just a matter of lifting out the old one and placing the new sink in the wooden framework under the wall faucets so the drain hole was immediately above the pipe leading straight down through the floor where the pipe ended and the water just soaked into the ground.

Our sparkling new white and green tile sink made the rest of the kitchen look dingy and dirty. I inquired about paint. Kimiko took me to a paint store where I bought a new type of Japanese paint and a brush. After Kimiko and Pappa-san moved everything out of the kitchen, I began painting the walls and ceiling white.

Kimiko and Pappa-san, all shook up because I was doing the painting myself, just stood watching me, shaking their heads and making their little hissing sounds. An audience of several more Japanese joined them to watch me paint. Kimiko told me they had never seen an American woman paint and didn't know we ever did that. I explained to her that many American women did their own painting as well as many other things along that line around their homes in the States, as everyone didn't have maids or houseboys there to do the work for them.

Seeing that I was really enjoying the work (I've always enjoyed painting), Pappa-san managed to come up with two more brushes from somewhere and he and Kimiko started helping me. The walls were so stained and discolored we had to put on two coats of white paint, but with their help in the small kitchen it didn't take us long to finish the job.

The freshly painted kitchen seemed to plead for new curtains. Kimiko and I took off again to a little nearby material shop where I found some cheap cotton yukata cloth, or summer kimono material, only eighteen inches wide, that suited perfectly. Little squares of bright red, green, blue and yellow were scattered over a white background. Instead of being able to buy whatever yardage I needed from a bolt of material, this yukata cloth was done up in parcels of the required yardage to make a kimono. This seemed like an awful lot of material for one small window, but I liked the pattern, it was cheap and, since it was so narrow, I wasn't sure how much it would take.

As it turned out I had more than enough with material left over, which gave birth to another idea. Since the storage space in our kitchen was so small and limited, I had Pappa-san build me a shelf, about twelve inches wide, and install it along the two walls above the window and door, about fifteen inches down from the ceiling. I hung material over this shelf rather than having doors installed. The shelves gave me a lot more storage space, the curtains made the kitchen more colorful, and the entire cost of remodeling was relatively inexpensive.

The one eyesore was the hot water heater, standing in the

little alcove of the kitchen. The heater and walls around it were blackened from smoke and dirt and was next to impossible to paint without disconnecting and removing the heater.

While I was racking my brain trying to figure out something to do about this dirty, ugly spot that could be seen not only in the kitchen but from the living room, Pappa-san came up with an idea of using a bamboo curtain. He cut it to just the right width to cover the opening, painted it white, and rigged it up with a little rope to roll the curtain up out of the way when we had to light the gas (it wasn't automatic), and have it down the rest of the time.

When Mr. Nokomura stopped by to collect the rent, Kimiko showed him the improvements in the kitchen, informing him I had paid for and done the work myself. He was sufficiently impressed that he had Kimiko figure up the cost of the sink and paint and deducted that amount from our rent.

Our redecorated kitchen, making living in private rental a little more bearable, started a chain reaction until each of our neighbors, one by one, had talked a new tile sink out of Mr. Nokomura.

45

Leaving the house one day I noticed dirty, filthy water oozing out of the ground near the garbage cans in the parking lot. I had no idea where it was coming from, but I had the passing thought that the ground under our houses must have become so saturated from our unique plumbing system that the ground was overflowing. That evening, when the fellas checked it, they came to the conclusion it must be from the cesspool.

The next day the seepage had infiltrated the parking lot, developing into a rivulet. I was aware of the foul odor, but it didn't disturb me anymore than the eternal smell of the honey buckets. However, it must have been different, as the natives walking or driving by our place carefully avoided the little stream of water that by then was not only in our parking lot but was running down the sidewalk.

On the third day the honey bucket men arrived, removed the lid and proceeded to empty the over-flowing cesspool. The process was a slow, tedious one. Using a very long handled wooden dipper, holding approximately a half gallon, they ladled the contents out into the buckets. The small, three-wheeled truck held about ten buckets and, when they were filled, they all drove off to empty them somewhere. The emptying of the cesspool took the most of one whole day and, once emptied, a couple of the boy-sans crawled down into it and scrubbed it down clean.

Knowing that human waste was sold in Tokyo to the farmers for fertilizer, I jokingly asked Kimiko to go out and ask the boy-sans how much okane they were going to pay me.

"Oh, Oku-san, I sink yours dame-dame. Taku-san water make dame-dame. I sink more better they put it in ocean. But if you say so, I speak."

But, of course, I was just kidding and I wouldn't let her go talk to the men.

46

School was out for summer vacation, and Jeanne and I enrolled Bonnie and Jeff in a riding academy at Camp Drake and signed them up for swimming lessons at the Grant Heights pool. A swimming lesson was given each morning, Monday through Friday, for six weeks, regardless of the weather. On mornings that it was too chilly to do much swimming, the instructors had the children go through various exercises to strengthen their muscles, develop deep breathing, and warm them up after a quick dip.

One rather warm week, Bonnie had a rash each time she finished her lesson. I took her to the dispensary and the doctor diagnosed it as heat rash. However, it only lasted a few days.

A week or so later, Jeanne learned there was a near epidemic of three-day measles going around and we guessed that's what Bonnie had. Thankfully, she had no ill effects from going swimming when she had the measles.

Weather permitting, we would all go back to the pool in the afternoon. The children thoroughly enjoyed swimming and playing in the water, plus they were around other children they missed with school out.

I vividly remember the afternoon it was my turn to stay with Nancy and Roddy at the baby pool while Jeanne was with Bonnie and Jeff in the regular pool. Wanting to get a good suntan, it occurred to me I would tan faster if I splashed water on me. I walked over to the baby pool and stepped into the water, hit the slippery bottom and lost my balance when my foot slid out from under me, and ker-SPLASH—there I was flat on my back in about six inches of water. Before I could get my arms and legs positioned to get out of the pool, I was further humiliated when a darling little three-year-old girl came up to me and, sticking her little face right up to mine, nose to nose, said, "Are you going swimming with us, too?"

After that embarrassing experience (and I can't swim!), I used sun tan oil to get my summer tan.

47

After reading about Nikko, I was convinced that somehow I had to finagle a trip there to see all the old shrines. I broached the idea to Jeanne and we discussed an opportune time, choosing the long weekend when the Fourth of July fell on a Monday.

Leerily we suggested the trip to Ed and Bill, but they surprised us by agreeing it was a good idea and helped us with our plans.

Situated up in the mountains ninety miles north of Tokyo, Nikko was easiest to reach by train. Ed got our tickets on a Japanese electric train and made hotel reservations through Special Services. Jeanne decided to take Hiroko, as this would give her an opportunity to go to her home near Nikko, plus she could help look after the children, see that we got on the right train and be our interpreter if we needed one.

Most of that Friday was spent in preparing food to take and packing clothes. Our train left downtown Tokyo at 7:30 a.m., and as Japanese trains are very punctual and wait for nothing or no one, we planned to leave very early to allow sufficient time for the long drive through traffic. Ed rounded up two staff cars with drivers for the nine of us plus our luggage. The cars arrived at 6 a.m., people and baggage were loaded, and we were on our way for our short vacation. But soon the cars pulled up and stopped in front of Shibuya, a big department store, and everyone got out.

"What are we stopping here for?" I asked.

No one answered me.

The drivers stacked our luggage there on the sidewalk and, seeing it all in a pile, it looked like we were going on a three-month tour. There were at least four large suitcases filled with summer and winter clothes, two picnic baskets of food, two long wooden cases containing fishing equipment, a flight bag full of liquor, two little shopping bags loaded with toys and books for the children, both families carrying a full supply of cameras and equipment; and Hiroko with her furoshika, a small square of material with the four corners tied together, containing her possessions.

We had a problem. How were we going to carry all of this luggage? Jeanne and I were trying to decide who should take what when Bill and Ed solved our predicament by locating a red-cap, who loaded all our things on a little cart. Hiroko told him our train number and destination and we followed him into this department store, up some flights of stairs (I was still asking why we were going in there, but no one paid any attention to me) until we reached the third floor. It looked exactly like a train depot with ticket booths, various check-out gates to several different tracks, and scads of people waiting.

We had arrived in plenty of time and, as is perfectly natural on any trip with children, they all had to go to the restroom. Hiroko led the way through the crowd to a big room opening off the waiting room. This room had no doors and once inside it was quite obvious it was a public restroom. Urinals and benjos on one side were separated by a small partition from more benjos on the other side; one side for women, the other side for men—no doors or walls, just that one slight partition. In the center were large wash basins, resembling our large, square drinking fountains found in public parks or school yards. A woman, stripped to the waist, was bathing at one. We located a vacant benjo at the far end, but poor Bonnie, at her overly modest age, just couldn't relieve herself under these conditions.

When we returned to the waiting room, our train was in and we could get on. Our red-cap had deposited our luggage at our assigned seats and we were soon speeding out of Tokyo into the country, which always fascinated me. Crossing over a bridge, we saw Japanese dyeing long lengths of cotton material in the river, discoloring the water a bright red. I would have liked to have gotten off the train to see how it was being done but, of course, that was impossible.

The train ride took several hours so we made good use of the picnic baskets, enjoying the fried chicken, sandwiches, pickles, potato chips, cookies, cokes and water. The Japanese undoubtedly thought we were gluttons with all of our food compared to their bowl of rice or dried fish.

The call of nature was urging quite strongly after Bonnie had eaten. She and I started down the train aisle in search of a restroom. Finding it, once inside this small room we both looked at the benjo; it was the first time either of us had had a really good look at one. We couldn't figure out which way to make an approach to this receptacle, and we started giggling. I told her it wouldn't make any difference, we were alone, just use it. But with the train swaying so roughly and the available handles in the wrong place, we both got to laughing so hard it was just another useless trip.

It wasn't too long before it became quite apparent that something would have to be done about Bonnie's predicament, so Bill took her to the restroom (which was perfectly proper as it was used by both men and women). After showing her the correct position to assume, and bracing her against the train's swaying, she finally got her much-needed relief.

In many places a toilet was just a hole in the ground or floor, but in the more modern stores, trains, etc., the hole was surrounded by a porcelain rim, possibly three to four inches high, with a little hood on one end (like a bottomless baby bassinet) and underneath was a receptacle, periodically emptied, and the contents sold to farmers. This porcelain rim, resting on the floor, was merely a decoration for the hole, thus necessitating a squatting position when used. The fancier benjos had a flush system, so it was important to know which way to face, otherwise one might get a shower! In the very elite places these benjos were decorated with little vases of fresh flowers. I do believe they have a good point or two. At least one doesn't have to worry about "occupying" a dirty seat, and they aren't too difficult to use once the proper stance is mastered.

The train was climbing the mountains and at one stop we had to decide whether to continue on the train winding around the mountains, or transfer to a cable car and go straight up. The fellas wanted to transfer and ride the cable car. The side of the mountain was quite steep. In fact, it was so steep each seat of the cable car was on a different level, stair-step style. Jeanne and the kids took one peek inside the car and decided they didn't want to ride. With the train gone and no other way to get up the mountain, we all got aboard, Jeanne literally crawling in, carefully sliding into the seat nearest the exit door, gripping the steel pole.

Up, up, up we went—and the view was positively breathtaking. At one point was a suspension cable car that went out over an abyss between the mountains and up to an observatory for an unobstructed view of Nikko National Park, but none of us were interested in that ride, believing our chances better on the cable car running on tracks than hanging up in mid-air over nothing. It was particularly exciting meeting the other cable car coming down.

"Hey, look," both Ed and Bill said from where they were standing at the front of the car.

"There's only one set of tracks and here comes another car." Bill said. "Maybe we'll have a head-on crash!"

Jeanne screamed, but at just the right moment the tracks divided into two tracks and we continued to the top without mishap. Upon our safe arrival at the end of the line, we practically knocked each other down getting out; however, Jeanne and I, with Hiroko's help, managed to see that the kids and luggage got off—the fellas taking care of themselves.

The little village was Hiroko's hometown and, meeting her parents was a little awkward for all as they didn't understand English and we couldn't understand them. Hiroko introduced each of us, and after much bowing following each introduction, she took us to the bus station for the last leg of our journey.

"Hey, how long you stay Japan, boy-sans?" Jeanne asked Ed and Bill, as typically Oriental they preceded us, having gotten on and off the various transfer points without lifting a finger to help us with the children or the luggage. By the time we loaded everything and everyone on the bus we were a little exasperated with them, plus a little tired of handling all that luggage.

The bus didn't have any springs and we bounced around worse than on any farm wagon I'd ever been on. The luggage kept falling off the racks until we stacked them in the aisles and on the seats so as not to get broken. As if the bouncing wasn't enough, the road began winding around the mountains and going higher with each turn; out of one hairpin curve right into another. The road looked only wide enough for one vehicle and, just to make the ride a little more thrilling, fog began settling in around us.

These conditions should have slowed our driver down, but apparently he was an ex-cab driver. He seemed to be pushing his foot down on the accelerator as hard as he was pushing on the horn, using only one hand on the steering wheel. I wouldn't let my self think what might happen if we met a vehicle. And Jeanne thought the cable car ride had been dangerous!

There were so many hairpin curves in that road I lost count. Besides being scared to death, jostled, bounced and disheveled until we felt like a piece of beef steak being tenderized, we all began asking, "Will this trip ever end? Will we arrive in one piece? Is this trip really necessary?"

At long last our mad bus ride came to an end. We arrived near the hotel grounds at Lake Chuzenzi, ten miles north of Nikko (more like ten miles straight up from Nikko). Once again the fellas managed to get just themselves off, leaving Jeanne and I to struggle with the kids and luggage. The bus had stopped at a little bridge, quite a distance to walk to the hotel, especially if we had to carry all the luggage. However, the hotel, expecting us, sent a boy-san to help us and show us to our rooms.

Lakeside Hotel, a Japanese hotel, had American or European style accommodations as well as Japanese accommodations. Not wanting to sleep on futons (nothing more than comforters on the floor) all weekend, our reserved rooms, across the hall from each other, had regular beds. Leys' room had three beds; our room had two large double beds, a table, two or three big rattan chairs, and lots of just space. One wall of the room was solid sliding glass doors that opened onto a hall or porch not more than six feet wide that was also solid glass sliding windows. Through all of this expanse of glass we had a wonderful view of the lake from the second floor of the hotel.

Jeanne and I were sorting out and distributing the luggage in the right rooms and the fellas, since they were on vacation, had to have a drink before they did anything. Ed discovered one of the bags was missing—the flight bag with all the liquor! Naturally, (from Ed), it was all the fault of Jeanne and me. We should have been more careful each time we unloaded and reloaded.

Quietly listening to his degrading remarks, plus Bill's added barbs, we got the final word in that it served them right for not helping us. After all, we were their American wives, not their hired maids.

Off they went in a huff down to the office to get us checked in, and see what they could find out about the missing bag. When they returned they were all smiles. With another tirade, they informed us that we (Jeanne and I) had left the bag at the bus terminal, but thanks to them (Ed and Bill) it would arrive on the next bus—and they (Bill and Ed) were right all along, there was nothing to worry about. MEN!!

Bill and Ed knew several other Americans from the Tokyo area who were to be at the lake that weekend, and they left to see who they could find they could talk out of a beer.

The children were anxious to get outside to see the sights and run off their excess energy after sitting for so long, and Jeanne and I were glad for some exercise and a breath of air, too.

The grounds around the large, rambling hotel were beautifully landscaped. A small mountain stream flowed along the edge of the hotel grounds emptying into Lake Chuzenzi. The lake, fifteen to eighteen miles in circumference, had several boats on it, both excursion and fishing boats. Inviting as the water looked, the pamphlets strongly advised against swimming since it was a mountain lake and the water was ice cold. The elevation here was 4,194 feet and the air was quite crisp.

Jeanne and I strolled through the small shopping district near the hotel and the large park, letting the children romp and play to their heart's content. Following signs in English that led up a little path toward Keggon Falls, we discovered an underground elevator to the bottom of the falls. We remembered our vow to never ride a Japanese elevator again, but when would we ever have a chance of seeing something like this again? It was too big of an opportunity to pass up, so with a quick look around and not seeing a single person near the elevator but us, we confidently bought tickets.

No sooner had we purchased them than it looked like school had just let out. Japanese children descended on us from all directions, each one buying a ticket and crowding into the elevator. Our courage deserted us; we gave up the trip and headed back to the hotel.

Bill and Ed had returned with another couple. It was supper time and we gathered in our room and finished off the remaining food in the picnic baskets. The fellas had retrieved Ed's liquor bag and, after bedding down the kids, we adults had a few drinks and played cards until we could no longer keep our eyes open and our minds on the game.

At breakfast the next morning we chanced eating in the hotel's dining room. After all, we'd been eating Japanese rice bread and eggs for some time and really enjoyed them. While dawdling over breakfast, we discussed our plans for the day with an older couple, Al and Mae Cabana, we'd met earlier. Al was a civil service worker the Leys had known for some time.

Our main reason for our trip was to see Nikko Park and this was the day for it. No one particularly relished the idea of riding the bus down the mountain around those hairpin curves, but it was the only way to get there. Jeanne and I were determined to visit the shrines, but Jeanne felt Roddie and Nancy were too young to enjoy the shrines and too little to withstand the strenuous day. That problem was soon solved when Bill and Mae offered to stay at the hotel and keep Roddie and Nancy entertained.

So Jeanne, Ed, Jeff, Al, Bonnie and I, well supplied with yen and camera equipment, bravely boarded the bus for the trip to Nikko. At the bus terminal, we transferred to a trolley to the shrine area. This was my first experience of riding a Japanese trolley. Every available seat was taken and we had to stand squashed between the passengers hanging onto the hand straps. But our ride wasn't too long.

We no sooner had gotten off when Al realized he'd left his camera and equipment on the shelf in the trolley car. Upset about the inconvenience, plus the amount of money this represented, he told us to go on and he would meet us at the shrines. As we headed toward the hallowed grounds, he was trying to convey his misfortune to a Japanese policeman.

Crossing the Daiya River by way of a brilliant red bridge, the Divine or God Bridge, put us on the path leading into the grounds. The view was positively beautiful. On either side of the path as far as we could see were extremely tall trees. This was Cryptomeria Avenue, its full length extending for twenty miles and the cryptomeria trees, originally numbering about forthy thousand in all, were planted in 1684. It was hard to believe that these beautiful trees were so old.

After a lengthy hike along this shaded lane, we emerged on the first of the shrines, which spread over a small part of the one hundred forty-one thousand acres of Nikko National Park. Such magnificence! This was how I had always visualized Japan would be:

The old, tall stately Peace Bell, or Sorinto Pillar, built in 1633 to keep the nation and the shrine area peaceful, which had been moved from its original site to its present location.

The beautiful five-story pagoda, brilliant red—the five tiled roofs representing earth, water, fire, wind and heaven, towering one hundred six feet high with a wooden pillar hanging inside to protect it from storms.

The sacred fountain with its twelve pillars of granite.

The colorful temple with the sculptured sleeping cat (carved by a left-handed sculptor) to keep the rats away.

The entrance gate to the Taiyobyo mausoleum which houses the grotesque, wild-colored God of Wind and God of Thunder.

The crimson and gold Yashamon gate with the four statues of Yasha (goblin who eats human meat and drinks human blood) protecting the temple.

The beautiful sacred Palanquin house with its glittering copper tiled roof, the whole edifice so delicately and intricately carved, gilded and lacquered.

The elaborate Yomeimon Gate, called "Day Spending Gate," because of the many carvings it is said it would take a full day to view and admire them all.

The sacred stable with the three lintels a series of monkey carvings depicting the life of man, one being the original carving of the three monkeys, "See no evil, speak no evil, hear no evil." (This was of particular interest to me, as I remembered how popular the three monkeys were in the United States before the War.)

There were so very many temples, shrines and gates—most of which were completely covered with carved designs, brilliantly painted in golds, yellows, reds, whites, and touched up with all the colors of the rainbow; the architecture topped off with the lovely sweeping curved tiled roofs. The structures, each an artistic masterpiece, separately situated among the timberland and hills, were connected by stairs, courtyards, roads or paths. All of this grandeur, leaving the beholder aesthetic, was further enhanced by the knowledge that these buildings were three to four hundred years old, yet were preserved and maintained so admirably.

Engrossed in sightseeing, we lost track of time until, tired from all our walking and climbing up and down stairs, we took advantage of a big courtyard with benches. Slipping off our shoes and wiggling our toes to restore circulation, we read our purchased brochures about the shrines. Jeanne called our attention to a commotion on the entrance stairs. An American, waving and motioning wildly, was being restrained by the gatekeepers from coming through the gate. Ed went to see what the trouble was and see if he could help a fellow countryman.

It was Al Cabana. We'd forgotten all about him. After Ed rescued him by paying his entrance fee and they rejoined us, Al told us that when he took off on his mad search for his camera he didn't have one bit of yen with him. Talking his way all the way to the entrance gate, after having retrieved his lost equipment, except for the little fracas at the gate, he knew he couldn't have returned to the hotel on "talk" alone, and it was too far to walk. He was unbelievably happy about finding us.

After our rest and rejoicing at the good fortune of being reunited with Al, we spent the rest of the day with more sightseeing and taking pictures until the sun disappeared behind the mountains and we headed back to the trolley, then to the bus, finally arriving at the hotel. It had been a long but most rewarding and awe-inspiring day.

About 3 a.m., the fellas got up quietly and went fishing. They hired a fishing boat with a skipper for this excursion. The flat-bottomed boat had one oar attached to the back and the Japanese skipper rowed it by standing on the back of the boat and paddling the one oar with the same actions a fish uses its tail.

Ed had complained that every time he went fishing, "some darn fool always has to take along some fishing poles." But it turned out their fishing trip was more leisure than actual fishing. Rod or pole fishing in Japan is just a matter of putting bait on the hook, and tossing the line into the water. Then just sit back, drinking beer or sake (to keep warm), wait for the ringing of the little bell tied on the line, and pull in the hooked fish. The fellas didn't have much luck, and they became chilled to the bones from the cold, night mountain air, but at least it was a new experience for them.

After Ed and Bill had a short nap and a good breakfast, they accompanied us to the park to see Keggon Falls. Clambering up a steep path, we reached the top of a cliff for our first full view of the falls. The view from this precipitous height was spectacular. The water gushed down the mountain for a three hundred thirty-foot drop, twelve little falls joining it near the bottom.

With our husbands along, we chanced the elevator ride to the bottom of the falls. This was a scary trip. The rickety elevator screeched and moaned on its slow descent, depositing us in a long, dark tunnel, the walls so damp that water was dripping from the sides and ceiling. Walking towards the sunlit exit, we found a concrete platform near the bottom of the falls where their height and beauty were even more dramatic.

The water cascading down into the deep ravine made sparkling silver streaks against the dark gray solid rock backdrop; the swirling spray, from the water being dashed against the rocks, was laden with rainbows. We spent quite some time drinking in all this beauty, prolonging our stay against the inevitable return trip by elevator.

Our short vacation was drawing to an end, and we returned to the hotel, repacked our clothes, and took a cab up the mountain further to lunch at Nikko Kanko, a hotel used exclusively by Americans and their dependents. The place was so crowded we had to wait in line for a table and we were slow in being served.

Then we had the bad luck of having to wait for a cab to return to the hotel. Getting a little anxious about the time, we grabbed our luggage and rushed to the office to check out of the hotel, only to learn that our bus had already left. The next bus would not leave in time for us to make connections with the train for Tokyo.

The only thing to do was to hire a cab and, luckily, Bill and Ed found one big enough for all of us. Away we went—speeding down that mountain, careening around those hairpin curves. Thank goodness I was squelched down in the middle of the back seat and couldn't see out of the windows, as I'm sure I would have been more scared than I was.

Our train was at the station upon our arrival at Nikko. Hiroko, patiently waiting for us, helped us get loaded. We stayed on the train all the way back to Tokyo, as none of us were up to transferring all the luggage and ourselves to the cable car and then back to the train, nor would our nerves have stood that trip again. The train trip was uneventful and we relaxed and rested as best we could.

On our arrival in Tokyo, the only available cabs at Shibuya Station were the little ten-yen cabs. Jeanne, Hiroko, Bonnie, Nancy and I, and part of the luggage, squeezed into one cab; and Bill, Ed, Jeff and Roddie, and the rest of the luggage, loaded into another cab. The cabbies knew we were all together and stuck close to each other, and then started racing towards our house.

About half-way home Nancy started fussing and wanted her bottle. It was in the other cab and Jeanne hollered to Ed to find it. Instead of pulling over to the curb so Jeanne could get the bottle, the cabbies made this race through traffic more exciting by pulling the cars alongside each other and, maintaining their breakneck speed with fenders rubbing so close they dislodged the accumulated dust, the bottle was passed from one car to the other. Riding in a race car in the Indianapolis 500 Speedway Race couldn't have been more thrilling. This wild ride seemed a suitable ending to our long weekend.

Later, when I read the fables and superstitions of Nikko National Park, recognizing some as pure fantasy yet aware of the plausibility of others, and having seen the old shrines that had remained untouched by any wars for so many years, combined with the experiences we'd had on our trip, I realized that things really worthwhile are never attained easily. I had to agree with the Japanese saying, "Never say Kekko (splendid) until you have seen Nikko." Truer words were never spoken.

48

Although we still had Tweedie Pie, the canary, and our gold fish (thank goodness the frogs were gone), Bonnie still wanted a pet she could play with. Kimiko offered to bring a puppy, but Bill said, "No."

One afternoon when Bonnie was visiting some friends at Grant Heights, they found an American family who had a mother cat with a litter of about five-week-old kittens they were wanting to give away. Bonnie really fell in love with them. That evening she begged for permission to get one. We'd never owned a cat and although Bill was quite sure he would never like a cat, he finally gave in and told her she could have one provided it was an American cat and not Japanese. We both assured him it was American as it had a long tail, not a bobbed tail.

The very next day I took Bonnie over to pick out her kitten. He was an adorable little gray and white spotted feline we named "Mittens." Bonnie spent many happy hours playing with him. He was so inquisitive, had to investigate everything and especially anything that moved. He was easy to housebreak and kept himself immaculately clean.

As he grew older, Bonnie would put him in the round dishpan and spin him around. When she stopped, he would crawl out and, trying to walk, would wobble and fall over, looking exactly as though he were pie-eyed drunk. Shaking his head to clear his vision, he'd crawl right back in the pan for another spin. If no one was around to spin him, he would knock over one of my little wicker wastepaper baskets, crawl inside and roll it around.

Gradually we let him spend more time outdoors and I soon learned the meaning of "something the cat drug in." He was forever finding something to play with and the first thing he would do was bring it inside—leaves, twigs, a crab, whatever. One of his favorites was catching an extra large praying mantis, three or four inches long. I'd never seen such big insects. He would carry one ever so gently with his teeth, never harming it, and turn it loose as soon as he was in the house.

Then ensued a battle of wits, speed and nimbleness to the end. The praying mantis would stand on its hind legs, weaving and dodging like a boxer as he fought with Mittens. Many's the time we ducked when a praying mantis leaped over us, with Mittens right behind him. Although I didn't particularly care for these creatures leaping around, it was fascinating to watch.

Mittens had two spots for taking his catnaps. If no one was around, or we were too busy to be bothered by him, he would curl up on top of our little radio. I don't know if he liked the warmth, or thought the vibration of the music was another form of purring. If anyone was sitting, he'd crawl up and drape himself about our shoulders. Mittens was so adept at sleeping in this position we could walk with him around our neck and he'd never fall. At times he would even leap to our shoulders from the ground, especially if strangers or a stray dog were around. He either didn't know Bill didn't like cats, or he was determined to win him over, as he'd crawl up on Bill the minute he got home from work and sat down to read the papers.

He had one peculiarity. Mittens would never drink water from a bowl. He preferred to go in the bathroom, stand on the rim of the bathtub and wait until someone would turn on the faucet and drink from the running water. When typhoon warnings were out and we knew the electricity would be shut off, we'd fill the tub so as to have water for various needs. Whenever that tub was full, Mittens would stand on the rim and drink from the water in the tub. It seemed every time that happened Bill was home. He just couldn't resist the temptation when he'd see Mittens precariously balanced on the tub rim with his little "fanny" sticking up—Bill just had to give Mittens a gentle push and in the water the cat would go. Mittens would no sooner hit the bottom of the tub than he came straight up, all four legs going as fast as they could, and he wouldn't stop until he'd find a place to get clean and dry.

Bonnie and I were mad at Bill the first time he did this, but Mittens didn't mind it particularly. He'd go right back for more; and he was always so soft and clean and fluffy after one of his dunkings he'd just strut.

Day after day he tried to catch the fish in the fish bowl. Walking around the bowl, he'd use a paw to scare the fish to the top of the water. When they were all at the top he'd leap to the rim and, balancing on three feet, he'd fish with one paw. The gold fish were too quick and too smart for him. He never did catch one. After several weeks of failure he finally gave up fishing.

I became concerned for the safety of Tweedie Pie and had Pappa-san build a bracket about two feet long to install above the window so the cage would hang away from everything. All went well until the afternoon when up the drapes Mittens climbed. Reaching the height of the cage, he made a leap for it. Bill had been watching him out of the corner of his eye and caught the cat in mid-air with a smack of newspaper. The bird cage was swinging dangerously high from the impact. The poor canary was so upset he not only lost some feathers trying to get out of the cage, but I thought he'd lose his voice from all the squawking noises. And Mitten's dignity was permanently damaged as far as the canary was concerned. He never again tried to attack the canary (at least when we were around), but would give Tweedie Pie lots of dirty looks when he was trying to nap and Tweedie Pie would be singing lustily.

The night I was trying to practice knitting—I'd taken only a few lessons and was really trying to concentrate on how to knit on a complicated Japanese knitting machine—I accidentally knocked a ball of yarn to the floor. Mittens pounced on it, rolling and chasing it all over the house. I'd seen pictures of kittens playing with yarn, but this was the first time I'd been involved. He played with that yarn, batting it around and under furniture, chasing, tumbling and rolling with it until he had completely unwound a three ounce skein of yarn. What he'd undone in less than an hour took me almost half a day to unsnarl and rewind.

Mittens became like a member of the family and he even convinced Bill that cats have personalities and are very likable and lovable. We wanted to bring him home with us, but the expense and trouble was more than a garden variety cat was worth, so we gave him to the family who moved into our house when we left Japan.

49

Partying at any of the Service Clubs was very nice, but I wanted to take in some of the clubs and restaurants in Tokyo. Reluctant to try this on our own, Jeanne and I started working on our husbands. Both of them had been in Japan before we arrived, and Bill had two previous tours in the Far East, so they weren't particularly anxious to go to the same places again. However, they surprised us one evening by announcing they were taking us out to dinner.

We went to Ketel's, a German restaurant on the Ginza. The small bar was on the first floor, and the dining room was in the basement, all typically German decor with Japanese waiters and waitresses. The German menu included such recognizable food as sauerbraten, wiener schnitzel, potato pancakes, split pea soup, and so on. The fellas ordered some German beer while we were making up our minds whether to show our ignorance by asking what the food was, or just close our eyes and point to something on the menu.

Jeanne suggested we each order a different dinner and switch the food around until we got something we liked. But Ed and Bill said that was dumb. They just looked over the food on the nearby tables and ordered by pointing to the dinner they thought looked good. As it ended up, we each had something different and got a taste of everything. The food, served directly from the utensil in which it was cooked, was steaming hot and most delicious. Enjoying ourselves immensely, Ed commented on the fact that here we were, four farm-raised Americans from the midwestern part of the United States dining in a German restaurant in the heart of Tokyo. Quite worldly!

50

One morning in July we were awakened by the pounding of drums, sounding louder and nearer than usual. The beating continued throughout the day and, with ominous persistency, the boom, Boom, BOOM reverberated through the night. By the next morning my eardrums were vibrating with each boom, and I told Kimiko it was so loud it would surely waken the dead.

"Hai, I sink so," she said, explaining that it was the three-day celebration of the O-bon Festival, or Feast of Lanterns.

Japanese lanterns are hung at the homes, Buddhist temples and bochis to light the way for spirits to find their way home for the annual reunion with their families. The favorite foods of the departed ones are placed on the altars. At the end of the three-day festival the food and lanterns are placed on rafts to float down the streams so the spirits may return to their "hereafter" with plenty of good food. The celebration is ended with the Bon-Odori or dance to help the participants overcome their melancholy.

When I went to a Buddhist temple near our house to take some pictures, I was surprised at finding Oji-san, the ichi-ban bamboo man, there. He recognized me and motioned for me to come up the stairs of the temple. Dressed all in white, shirt and short pants, he introduced me to the gentleman with him and, after much bowing, they posed for me to take their picture. Then, chattering in Japanese, he proudly showed me the decorations and beautiful food arranged on the altar. I was sorry I couldn't understand him, as I would have liked to have learned more about this festival. I couldn't fathom how Japan, with its problem of feeding its over-populated country, could afford to be so lavish with food for the spirits. Just more proof that it was utterly impossible for an American to understand an Oriental's way of thinking.

The rest of that summer seemed like one long celebration. The Japanese celebrate approximately forty major festivals a year. Some parts of Japan use the regular calendar; others the lunar calendar, or about one month later. From reading various articles, combined with Kimiko's versions, I learned that many of the festivals originated around 500 B.C., some just small affairs of paying homage to a patron deity where some historical or mythical miracle or apparition happened; others, quite elaborate with costumes and decorations, last for several days. The Buddhist always burn incense during their celebrations, and the Shinto decorate with white paper and straw ornaments.

The Tanabata, or Romantic Festival, is celebrated on the seventh day of the seventh month, honoring the two loving stars, Altair and Vega, who meet for one night a year across the heavenly river, the Milky Way, providing it is a clear night. If it is cloudy, the two lovers must wait another year. The children decorate bamboo trees with little pieces of colored paper upon which they write their wishes, and the next day the trees are tossed in the nearest river so they will float into heaven carrying the messages to the star lovers.

Doyo-no-ushi, Day of Summer Ox, which is supposed to be the hottest day of summer by the old calendar, is celebrated by the participants eating broiled eel and rice.

The Sichi-Go-San Festival for all girls seven, five and three. These girls dress in elaborate silk kimonos and tour certain temples with their parents and friends.

Otave-Matsuri, Aki-Matsuri and O-Matsuri, in the spring, summer and fall, all pertain to the rice crop—celebrating the first transplanting of the seedlings, first harvest and so on—and were of Shinto origin. The Omikoshi, or large gold palanquin, balanced on the shoulders of several men and boys dressed in white pants and colorful happi coats, or just loin cloths, head a parade of women and children. The palanquin bearers, repeating an unintelligible chant, dance with a twisting and turning as though to test the strength and agility of the others not to lose their footing or drop the palanquin. Some are liquored up from drinking sake. They eat raw fish to keep up their strength. All motor traffic stops when one of these parades is on a main thoroughfare. The paraders, in their boisterous pleasure, can dart from one side of the street to the other with its unplanned twisting progress.

By the Oriental Zodiac, the year we were there was the year of the Hitayi, or sheep, and this was depicted by fortune tellers and astrologers by pictures of a goat. From what I could learn, sheep and goats are scarce in Japan and thus the true likeness was often misrepresented.

There were many, many other festivals, and much of the information I gathered was rather confusing. I had the definite impression that even the participants weren't sure of the real reason for the celebration, having maintained the festivals for so many years, but were just captivated by the infectious gaiety of it all—much like we Americans who celebrate Christmas with Santa Claus and cocktail parties, forgetting the real meaning of Christmas.

Although these festivals seemed strange to me, I'm sure that any Japanese, spending a year in America, would find many of our celebrations strange to them and hard for the Oriental to understand, such as St. Valentine's Day, Halloween, St. Patrick's Day, and our other holidays. So maybe, I thought, we aren't so different basically after all.

51

When a pilot friend of the Ley's spent a weekend with them on leave from Korea, the five of us went night-clubbing. We started out at a recently opened club called the Latin Quarter. It was a huge place with a low ceiling and the only lighting was low-burning candles on each table. These tables, jammed as close together as possible, spread over a space that looked as big as the "back forty."

We enjoyed a good floor show, accompanied by an excellent Japanese dance band, and could hardly keep from laughing hilariously when a darling young Japanese girl, billed as having just completed a successful tour of the United States, sang "Lover" with all her "l's" sounding like "w's."

Whenever a drink was half gone a nearby boy-san refilled it without asking what we were drinking. The minute anyone pulled out a cigarette, he was right there with a lighter. And, each time he approached our table he insisted he could get a jo-san, or girl, for our pilot friend.

We had no idea how much all of this was costing. Figuring our bill could run up pretty fast, like the national debt, we decided to make a quick trip to the latrine and then go someplace else. Jeanne and I went first. The walls of the ladies' powder room were solid mirrors and lovely little pink velvet cushioned boudoir stools were placed near the built-in vanity circling the room. This vanity ledge was lavishly furnished with combs, brushes, lipstick, powder and cologne. The latrine section offered a choice of Japanese benjos as well as Western style toilets.

When the fellas came back from their trip, they reported they thought they'd gone in the wrong door at first, as it looked exactly like a flower shop. The male patron could purchase any kind of flower or have a corsage of his choice made up for his lady fair. With all this extra service we knew we'd better get out of there, so the fellas asked for the bill. To this day I don't know how much it cost; but I do know it was so expensive it cleaned all three of the guys of the yen they had and they said we'd have to drop by the Service Club so they could pick up some more yen before we went anywhere else.

After stopping at one of the U.S. Service Clubs where they got more yen, we went to a couple of other bars, ending up at a small one with only a few booths, a tiny dance floor and an accomplished pianist providing good music. There were only a few people there and it was so quiet compared to the others. We sat at the bar, enjoying the music and chatting with the bartender. Jeanne and I decided we'd had enough to drink, so we ordered a mizu-frappe (incorrect in any language). The bartender "ah-soooed," and, laughing at our little joke, served us water over ice—just what we wanted.

52

As each of our excursions into the unknown had proved more interesting, Jeanne and I gained more confidence with each trip. We were learning more Japanese words, and Jeanne knew most of the main streets in Tokyo. With the aid of a map we felt capable of going any place without getting lost. We'd heard so much about the wholesale market in Tokyo and especially of the material shops, we were determined to find it. With me driving and Jeanne acting as navigator (in the suicide corner), we headed for the Ginza.

Ginza Street could be compared with Halstead Street in Chicago or Canal Street in New Orleans. Shops along the Ginza sell all kinds of items from the ridiculous to the sublime, prices varying from the very cheapest to the most expensive. Many shops had "barkers" trying to sell their wares. In some instances, the shopkeepers would literally pull prospective customers in off the street in an attempt to make a sale. The street, shops, salespeople, customers and just sightseeing produced a carnival-like atmosphere.

During our jaunt along the Ginza we found a shop selling Japanese school outfits in which several young school boys were working. Since most Japanese school boys spoke English fairly well, we went in for directions to the wholesale district, which we were sure was nearby.

Upon entering the store we were met by a young lad who bowed low to us, saying, "Ohayo gozaimasu."

Returning the greeting, Jeanne asked, "Do any of you boys speak English?"

"Hai, sukoshi."

She asked for the directions to the wholesale district. The more she talked, the more confused the poor lad became. Realizing she was getting nowhere, she asked me to try.

He interrupted with, "Gomen nasai. Chotto matte kudasai," and walked to the rear of the store to converse with the other Japanese clerks who had gathered to watch us. After a prolonged conversation and many glances our way, another boy came forward.

Speaking slowly, I asked, "Do you understand English?"

"Hai, sukoshi."

"We are looking for a material store with takusan material, you understand?"

Sucking air in through his teeth, he answered, "Hai, sukoshi."

So I went through a series of gestures to portray the word "material" and kept repeating the word as I touched my blouse and Jeanne's blouse. Suddenly his face lit up and he said, "Ah so!" and beckoned us to follow him. We didn't understand this, but we followed and he led us to the counter where shirts were displayed.

"Iie, iie," we both chorused, shaking our heads negatively. I pretended to get a bolt of material down from the shelf and, working my fingers like scissors, acted as though I were cutting something out.

When I started this routine, the first boy joined the second, and after another lengthy conversation, they walked to the front of the store. Following them, we watched as they pointed down the Ginza. We listened intently, but could only recognize some names of train stations. Apparently they didn't know we had a car, and were directing us to wherever they thought we wanted to go by train. When they'd finished, we departed with a "Domo arigato goramasu."

These train stations could be tucked in a store, underground, or any other unlikely place. We didn't know if they were relevant or not as we weren't convinced the boys understood us anymore than we'd understood them. So we got in the car and took off in the general direction they had pointed.

Driving around and around in an ever-widening circle, still looking for the material shop, we'd about given up when we spotted an interesting street we hadn't seen before. Again I parked the car and we took off on foot.

Our first stop was a large rattan shop. Jeanne discovered she could get fiber rugs, made up in squares, so she got the name of the store and price of the rug so she could tell Ed about it; and we went on our way. It was a fascinating street with varied wares where everything was done up in packages of one dozen or more. Few of the shop keepers could speak English. We'd found the wholesale district, but not the material shop. Locating a shop with all kinds of Christmas decorations, we purchased several items at fabulously low prices.

Although tempted to wander further down this little narrow road, so much time had already been used up and, aware that we were the only Americans on the street, we decided to return to the car.

We checked the map to see where we were so we'd know what road to get on. This was no small problem with the roads in Tokyo winding around as they do. Our return journey planned, we took off, but somewhere I must have missed a turn or Jeanne read the map wrong.

"Quick, Geil, turn around," she excitedly warned me. "We're off the map!"

Experience had taught me I couldn't drive around the block, so to keep from getting lost I made a U-turn to "get back on the map" so Jeanne could direct us home. We never found the material store we were looking for that day, but it was an episode we enjoyed and we saw some of Tokyo we probably wouldn't have seen otherwise.

Jeanne asked me one evening if I would help her make plans for a shower and pick out a gift for one of Ed's sergeants. He'd been back in the States on emergency leave because he'd lost his wife when his house and all their belongings had been destroyed by fire, and had just returned to Japan with his two sons.

"Isn't that a strange coincidence," I told her. "We just recently received the Rantoul Press, our hometown newspaper, and it contained an article about a schoolmate of mine. The same thing happened to him, and he's stationed in Japan."

"Maybe it's the same. Something like that doesn't happen everyday, right down to every detail. What's his name, your schoolmate?" Ed asked.

"Do you really think it's the same?—Warren Fisk, from Rantoul. But I haven't seen or heard of him since we graduated from high school in 1938."

"Well, how about that. Sgt. Fisk works for me and he's the one we're having the shower for. I didn't know he was from Rantoul. You and Bill will have to come to the party, too. Okay?"

Ed Ley made arrangements with Mr. Nokomura to get the next available house, and Warren Fisk and his two boys moved in two doors from us. His sons, Russell, about the same age as Bonnie, and Jerry, a year or two older, spent a lot of time at our house during the rest of the school vacation while their Dad was at work.

53

Bonnie and Jeff Ley had taken riding lessons during the summer and fall and Mr. Yamada-san decided they were good enough to be in the Imperial Palace Horse Show, an annual event. We parents were as excited about getting into the Palace Grounds as we were about the children being selected to ride in the horse show.

Jeanne bought some material and had the tailor make Jeff a smart riding outfit—black jodhpurs, a bright red wool English-style riding jacket and cap. I fashioned a pair of jodhpurs for Bonnie from Bill's old khaki trousers, with which she wore her black riding boots and a white sweatshirt.

The day of the show was sunny, although there was the hint of autumn in the air. Our spirits high, we left early so we'd be sure to arrive in time for Bonnie and Jeff to be registered and coached on what to do. What a thrill crossing the moat and entering the Palace Grounds. I'd hoped to tour the whole palace once inside, but we were permitted only on certain roads and in certain areas in connection with the horse show. The rest of the grounds were strictly off limits, and guards were stationed all about to see that no one intentionally or unintentionally wandered into the forbidden areas.

The Palace race track, stables and jumps were decorated with bright colored banners. Fancy tents, red and white awnings and canopies sheltered the various seating arrangements. All of this grandeur, plus the scenic background against the high gray stone walls, gave me the feeling we'd gone backwards in time to King Arthur's days. Captivated by the beauty of the grounds, enhanced by the wealthy and royal Japanese ladies in their beautifully printed silk kimonos, the worldly "horsey set" in their distinguishable chic outfits, dignitaries of foreign countries dressed in their own colorful native attire, plus Americans, all kept me agape.

The superb array of horses, all purebreds, had been groomed until they literally glistened. In fact, the horses Bonnie and Jeff were riding had come from Emperor Hirohito's private stables, each horse having earned his own claim to fame.

Settled in our assigned seats, we watched the racing and jumping events, and then Jeff's class made its appearance. The students and horses went through their routines as though they were all pros, with one exception. When they were lined up for the presentation of awards, Jeff's horse bucked, causing Jeff to somersault right over the horse's head! However, he landed on his feet, neither dropping the reins nor losing his cap, and ended up getting first place in his class.

Next Bonnie's class started its routine. About two-thirds of the way through the exercise, the horse behind Bonnie's started crowding and suddenly nipped Bonnie's horse on the rump. Startled, he reared on his hind legs and, with nostrils flaring, stretched out his legs full length and took off like a bolt of lightning! My heart did a double flip. I was afraid Bonnie couldn't stick on him and would be thrown and seriously hurt. But she bent forward over his neck, stuck like glue, and pulled on the reins until she had him under control. They returned to the group and finished the exercise.

Much relieved for her safety, Bill and I appreciated the round of applause she received. At least that was something for her efforts. However, the judges, who'd witnessed her wild ride, awarded her fourth place and she was presented a bronze medal. Added to her charm bracelet, it's a constant reminder of her day at the Imperial Palace Horse Show in Tokyo.

54

Kimiko discovered a lump in her upper lip that fall. She told me it didn't hurt, just annoyed her. We watched it for several weeks, but it grew larger, becoming an ugly dark purple color. It looked like a bloody tumor or cyst to me. I suggested she go to a doctor about it.

Her doctor didn't know what it was, but told her what he thought it might be. I couldn't find an English word for the Japanese name he'd given her. On her second visit to the doctor, he told her he thought he should operate. She was visibly shaken by this and told me I'd better find a new maid.

"Don't you worry about us, Kimiko. You go to the hospital and have that taken care of, and when you feel like coming back to work you've got a job with us. If not, we'll worry about that when the time comes."

The following Monday she returned to work. She thought her husband's hospital insurance covered her, but it was only for himself and his father. She worked for us that week while financial arrangements were made so she could go to the hospital. Friday, she told me not to expect her back. Before she left, she said long, tearful goodbyes to Tweedie Pie, the goldfish, cuddled Mittens as she talked to him, and lastly to each of us.

"Kimiko, do let us hear from you," I said as we walked to the bus with her. "Come back and see us when you get well, OK?"

"Hai, I do. Sayonara, Oku-san, Sayonara, Serlgeant. Sayonara, Bonnie-chan," she said, giving Bonnie a loving hug.

She got on the bus, all of us waving until the bus disappeared around a corner. That was the last we ever saw or heard of Kimiko. We didn't have her home address, nor did we know anyone who knew her. Pappa-san and Hiroko inquired around, but could learn nothing. Kimiko left an emptiness in our home that was never filled.

After a few weeks, when I was finally convinced she wasn't coming back, I hired a boy-san to come in once or twice a week to do the cleaning and laundry; otherwise, I did my own work. And when Bill was gone on a trip, Bonnie and I would spend the night at Jeanne's.

It was never the same without Kimiko. There's a special little place in our hearts just for her, and whatever happened to her, or wherever she might be, I hope she knows how very much she meant to us all.

55

In spite of the honey buckets, we'd drive through the country at least once a month to follow the methods of farming—from the preparation of the soil in the spring through the last harvest in the fall. The diligence, patience and cooperation of each member of the farm family made it possible for them to raise and produce several crops from their small, postage-stamp size fields.

Wading in mud, the farmers cultivated the flooded fields with crude garden tools, leading an ox pulling a wooden plow, or by pushing a mechanized plow looking similar to our power lawn mowers. The rice seedlings, removed from the homemade greenhouses, were tenderly set in the muddy ground, and the flooded fields were constantly watched to control the proper depth of the water during the early part of the growing season.

Seeds, such as corn, beans, wheat, etc., were sowed by hand by one member of the family in a row made by another by stamping his bare feet in the soft earth; or plants or seedlings were set by one in a shallow trench made with a hoe by another; and a third member of the family raked the soil over the seeds or plants.

Before the first crop was harvested, another crop was

planted in between the growing plants so one little plot of ground had a constant procession of two different grains or vegetables in alternating rows. This method probably more than doubled the yield from their land.

Plants producing their crop above the surface, such as cabbages, or whose flowering blossoms affect the vegetables, such as potatoes, and any fruit-bearing bushes or trees whose fruit was still in the formative stage, were all carefully guarded against frost, insects, wind or rain damage by a protective covering of rice paper. It was a strange sight to be driving along a country road and see an apple tree with what appeared to be balls of paper hanging from its limbs instead of apples. No wonder their fruits and vegetables were so beautiful in the markets when they received such tender loving care.

Harvesting, as in most of their farming, was done by hand. Carrots, carefully dug out of the ground, were tied in bunches; tops cut off and scrubbed until they glistened. Somehow they managed to dig up three foot-long carrots without breaking them (we'd buy one of these long carrots for the horses when Bonnie and Jeff had a riding lesson).

Daiku was hung up on bamboo poles or tree limbs before taken to market. Wheat and rice were cut by a hand sickle, tied in bundles, and the grain was either stamped out by feet or by using a hand harvesting machine transported from house to house by the operator on his bicycle; or, in the more thickly populated areas, the grain was taken to a small mill. The chaff was removed by pouring the seeds from one wicker container to another and letting the wind carry it away. The straw was woven into mats used to spread the grain on the ground for drying, made into raincoats and hats for the farmers, put on the backs of oxen and cows as a protection from the rain or hot sun; sacks for transporting grain, charcoal, and other items; fitted covers for breakable bottles and jars; soles of getas; and for many, many other uses.

On one excursion into the country, we were invited into the courtyard of several homes. Instead of a grassy lawn, the whole yard was nothing but hard packed earth, immaculately clean with not a leaf, twig or even a blade of crabgrass in sight. A few large odd-shaped stones were placed in the otherwise clean-swept enclosure. Beautiful potted chrysanthemums, growing possibly five or six feet high topped with huge blossoms, were lined up in front of each house. A dead crow, tied to a wooden post above the flowers, was a warning to keep the birds away.

The three or four mamma-sans and several little children, none of whom could speak English, made us feel welcome. Dressed in dark printed, long blousy pants, wrap-around blouses, with bright printed quilted hip-length jackets to protect them from the autumn chill, they seemed to enjoy scrutinizing us as much as we did them.

We all watched as approximately fifty girls, about twelve or fourteen years old, dressed in white middy blouses and navy blue bloomer shorts, raced past on the dusty, dirt road. The weather was quite chilly, but the racing girls must have felt like it was one hundred degrees in the shade. Some were covered with perspiration, others looked nearly exhausted with their faces flushed as they panted for breath. They must have run quite a distance, and still continued running on past us out of sight.

This racing and running was an integral part of the Japanese school system. It seemed this strenuous physical education apparently counter-balanced their poor diet to keep them healthy and strong, capable of walking long distances, working long hours, and in general withstanding bodily fatigue.

56

Without any prodding from us, Bill and Ed asked us out for dinner. It was a good thing I didn't know where we were going or I wouldn't have gone. Being a meat-potatoes-and-gravy gal, I didn't care for strange and exotic foods, and particularly the

Oriental foods. So wouldn't you know—they took us to a Chinese restaurant!

A Geisha-type girl met us and escorted us up a narrow, steep stairway to a private dining room containing four chairs around a large round table with a built-in Lazy Susan. The table and chairs were lower than our American furniture. The fellas did the ordering as I silently hoped they'd get something I could eat. A small dish, about the size of a saucer, a large china spoon with a short handle, a bowl about half the size of a dessert dish, and chopsticks were set before each of us.

"They must be kidding," I said. "I'm starved, and these little dishes won't hold nearly enough for me."

"Don't get excited, Geil," Ed told me. "There's no law that says you can't refill your plate as many times as you want. If you don't get enough to eat here, we'll go get you a hamburger or steak someplace."

"Okay, I may take you up on that because I won't eat bird's nests or rotten eggs."

Our waitress started bringing in the food, placing it on the Lazy Susan—slivered green beans, shredded beef, walnut halves dripping in a sweet sauce, bite-sized pieces of chicken deep fat fried, Chinese egg rolls with a shrimp and rice filling, and soy sauce.

"C'mon, Geil, try some. Take some chicken on your plate, put some soy sauce in your bowl, and use your chopsticks to dip each bite in the sauce before you eat it."

"I can't work these things," I said, fumbling with the chopsticks. "Jo-san, dozo, may I have a fork?"

"Hai," she said and with a low bow the waitress backed out of the room.

Jeanne, Ed and Bill started eating. The waitress didn't return. So picking up the chopsticks, I placed them between the fingers of my right hand like the others and tried to pick up a piece of chicken. One or the other of the chopsticks would slip and pop out of its position and the chicken kept sliding around on the plate. Anchoring the chicken with my left hand,

I tried again. Success! About three inches from my mouth, the chopsticks slipped, flipping in opposite directions, and the chicken went sailing to the floor. Boy, was I glad we were in a private dining room.

"Where's that waitress with my fork?" I said and disgustedly retrieved the chicken from the floor just as she re-entered. "Jo-san, dozo, may I have a fork, please?"

And again she said, "Hai," as she backed from the room.

"Do you suppose she doesn't understand me?"

"She probably does," Bill answered, "but she won't let on that she does. You're not going to get a fork. Use your chopsticks, and quit complaining."

I tried. Oh, how I tried. I'd seen Kimiko eat everything from one small grain of rice to spaghetti with her chopsticks, but danged if I could get the hang of how those things worked. After several unsuccessful attempts and losing more food on the floor, I finally threw down the chop sticks and said, "I give up, I can't work these darn things. If I can't have a fork, you'll just have to excuse me because I'm going to use my fingers. I'm hungry."

The food was good, but a little of it went a long way. The soy sauce, the greasy sweetness of the walnut meats and egg rolls, and the deep fat fried food was too rich for me. My struggle with the chopsticks, however, convinced me why the Japanese furniture was low and why the dishes are small. By holding a bowl in the left hand the chopsticks in the right hand, it cuts down on the distance the food travels, thereby reducing the risk of losing it.

57

The tailor and his wife, whose combination shop and house were near us, had done quite a bit of sewing for Jeanne as well as had helped me with some of my sewing problems. During a conversation with Mamma-san, the tailor's wife, she mentioned she'd never been in an American home. Jeanne suggested that it would be a nice gesture to show them our homes sometime. When Ed learned about it, he wanted to make an evening of it and show the many colored slides he'd taken in Japan.

Since Jeanne's quarters were larger than ours and more "American," she invited them over one evening. We picked up the tailor and his wife and drove them to Grant Heights. Japanese weren't allowed in the housing area unless accompanied by Americans or employed there.

Ed had the screen and projector set up and, after giving the Japanese couple a tour of the house. Ed, being a typical American host, asked everyone what they would like to drink. Pappa-san, the tailor, didn't speak English, but his wife spoke it fairly well, having learned it from American GIs.

Ed told her he had American whiskey or, if Pappa-san preferred, he even had sake. She related the message to Pappa-san, and then told Ed he would prefer whiskey. She said Pappa-san drank too much sake all the time, and one time she had told him she wasn't going to buy him any more liquor to drink. Then she started laughing and said, "He got takusan 'peesed' off and he speak, 'No sake, no workee.' So now he get sake. But tonight he want whiskey."

After a pleasant evening of viewing the slides, visiting and drinking, Pappa-san and his wife were so grateful for the unusual evening we could hardly get them to stop bowing and saying, "Domo arigato."

When we arrived back at our parking lot, I'll swear they both backed all the way to their place, bowing and thanking us. In fact, Pappa-san got to bowing so low I was afraid he would scrape his head in the gravel.

It gave Jeanne and me a good feeling about entertaining a Japanese family, as I think they really enjoyed it. I honestly believe that if more people tried to learn the home life and customs of foreigners and let them see and learn ours, and gain an understanding and respect for each other's, it would be a big step forward in human relations and world peace.

58

To be sure our gifts arrived in the States by Christmas, we shopped early so they could be mailed in early November. Consequently, we purchased the gifts for our immediate family early, leaving more time to enjoy the pre-Christmas parties and events.

"Dusty" Rice, a great football player from someplace in Iowa, and his family became our neighbors, as well as another football player on the Air Force team, so we became avid football fans that fall and winter. I've always enjoyed football games, and these were particularly good as the teams were made up of top players from U.S. colleges and pro-football players. The added attraction of the Jodie Drill Team was well worth the time spent at a game if one didn't like football.

The members of the drill team were volunteer airmen who had practiced their marching routine to such a degree of precision that when the order was given to "freeze," all members of the squad could stop in mid-step, looking like a movie film had been stopped, hold their stance motionless, with all legs, feet, heads and arms of the men in the same position, until the next order was given. Although their style of marching wasn't top military style, being more of a shuffling dance step than brisk marching, it was so unique and clever and combined with their sing-song chanting, the squad became well-known all over the Far East and even back in the States.

Before the game on Bonnie's birthday, Dusty and Jerry both promised Bonnie they'd make a touchdown just for her as their birthday gift to her. And by golly, they both kept their word! The Air Force team defeated Navy and earned the right to play the final game for top team in the Far East.

The playoff, Army vs. Air Force, was at Meiji Stadium on December 31. The air was nippy, perfect football weather, and a large crowd of Japanese and Americans filled the stadium. The opposing sides seemed to try to out-do the other in decorations, pre-game entertainment and noise. The Army Band, Air Force Band, a Scottish Bagpipe Corps, crack rifle teams, Jodie's Drill Team, a Chinese dragon, the Army mule, all kinds of fireworks, bombs and balloons—there were so many things going on that one just didn't dare blink his eyelids or something would be missed.

It was a terrific game! Each time a score was made a volley of aerial bombs was set off. (At first I wasn't sure if they were celebrating the touchdown, or if they were trying to blow the overhead helicopters right out of the sky.) When a yellow hankie was dropped because of a foul or illegal procedure, the spectators started singing (to the tune of "London Bridge Is Falling Down") "There's a hankie on the play, on the play, on the play. There's hankie on the play. Ah, so deska."

We were all so proud of Dusty's superb playing. Although each time he was tackled Jo, his pregnant wife, would jump up and yell at the Army player not to hurt him; and she did so much jumping up and down we were afraid she'd have her baby right there in the stands. But thanks to Dusty, the Air Force won the game and he was carried off the field by his teammates.

For winning the game, the Air Force team members and their wives were awarded a weekend's stay in the Imperial Hotel, and we were invited to drop in after the game for a drink.

This beautiful hotel, used almost exclusively by tourists visiting Japan, was filled with celebrating Americans. No sooner had we arrived at Dusty's room than a beautiful kimono-clad Japanese girl brought in a bottle of champagne, compliments of the hotel. Team members, wives and well-wishers were darting from room to room, toasting each other with Bill acting as bartender in Dusty's room, dispensing the champagne and liquors.

Dusty hadn't had a chance to shower and clean up after the game and, after a few drinks and even with his room full of people, he had to have a hot bath. After he'd removed his jersey and pads, everyone had to check his back to see how badly he'd been injured when an Army player had run across his back, his cleats tearing Dusty's shirt and ripping his back. Then he submerged himself in a sunken tub that looked like a small swimming pool.

We had a New Year's Eve party to attend and when I noticed it had grown dark outside, we took our leave. The maid I'd hired to stay with Bonnie was waiting for us; she and I borrowed a cot from the neighbors for her to sleep on, and I got dressed for the party.

Bill had lain down for a short nap while I was attending to these duties. When I tried to waken him, first by calling to him and then shaking him, I realized he was out cold. He must have sampled every drink he mixed. It's a good thing I hadn't known he was drunk when he was driving us home through all that traffic. I knew I could never get him awake, sobered up and dressed to go to the party. We returned the borrowed cot, I dismissed the maid, and I went to bed, too. I'd had about enough excitement and celebration for that New Year's Eve.

59

Because of the football game on Bonnie's birthday, we had a party for her the night before. Her guests arrived after school for a buffet supper, and Donna was invited to spend the night, as we weren't about to go through the experience of trying to take her home again.

I'd found a picture in a stateside magazine of a beautiful birthday cake—a small doll standing in the center of an angel food cake with the cake decorated to look like the doll's ruffled hooped skirt—and I'd taken the picture and a doll to the Grant Heights bakery a week early and ordered the birthday cake.

Everything was ready the day of the party except pick up the cake. It was to be ready at four o'clock, but since I was in the commissary right after lunch I thought I might pick it up and save myself an extra trip. The Japanese boy-san I talked to knew absolutely nothing about my order and said they didn't have such a cake. This really floored me, as I'd ordered it a week before. I asked to speak to the manager. The boy-san called another Japanese boy-san, and they went into a long discussion in Japanese. Patiently I waited until they were finished, and the second boy-san informed me that yes, they had my order, but I had the wrong day. It would be ready the next day.

This really threw me in a rage and I demanded to see the man in charge of the bakery. They just stood and looked at me. I told them I had to have the cake that day, not the next day. I was so upset my voice was getting louder and I could feel my face getting redder by the minute as everyone in the commissary stopped what they were doing and watched me. If there had been any other way or place to get a birthday cake, I think I would have tried to quietly slip away.

When the Army sergeant in charge of the bakery came out and wanted to know what the trouble was about, I told him of my problem. I explained I'd ordered the cake a week ago and they'd promised to have it ready for me. Fighting to hold back my tears, I told him that because of this silly misunderstanding my little girl wasn't going to have a birthday cake.

He listened attentively, then asked one of the boy-sans how long it would take him to decorate a cake for me. The boy-san stood there sucking air in through his teeth until I thought I'd scream, and then he said, "Oh, maybe thirty minutes, but not be so pretty." That was fine with me. Any kind of a cake would be better than none at all.

So much time had elapsed that I mentioned to the sergeant that the commissary would be closed before the cake would be ready. He assured me I'd still get my cake, and told me to come back later to the back door to pick it up. I thanked him from the bottom of my heart, and as I left I heard him barking orders to the boy-san to get started on my cake.

When I returned, after having had time to calm down and

wishing I'd just gotten a plain cake and decorated it myself, I half-heartedly knocked on the back door of the commissary. The sergeant opened the door; said the cake was ready and asked me to step in and see it. It was beautiful! If this was a "not-so-good job" I can't imagine what his best work would be like. It not only looked exactly like the picture, but better. I was extremely happy and conveyed my thanks not only to the sergeant but to the boy-san who did the decorating, and we all apologized to each other for the misunderstanding.

The party was a huge success. The girls had good, healthy appetites and devoured the ham, baked beans, potato chips and salad. The cake was a complete surprise to all, and they almost didn't want me to cut it. Bonnie received many nice gifts, and will always remember it as one of her favorite parties, because it had such varied guests: Christian, Jewish, Hawaiian, Nisei and Negro—all just happy little girls celebrating a birthday.

60

Jeanne had entertained us for Thanksgiving dinner and, although I'd hoped to be in quarters and better equipped for entertaining, we decided to have the Christmas dinner. For fear the electricity would go off, I started my preparations the day before so I could bake the pie crust before roasting the 15-18 pound turkey in Jeanne's electric roaster.

This was the first time I'd ever stuffed a turkey and I wasn't sure how much dressing it would take. I made up enough to fill a big dish pan. Dusty Rice stopped by just then and asked me to help Jo, his wife, make dressing and show her how to stuff their turkey. I confessed my ignorance and told him that I'd help Jo, but it would probably be like an amateur American trying to demonstrate the Japanese tea ceremony to a novice.

When Dusty saw the trouble I was having hanging on to that slippery bird, he picked it up and, tucking it under his arm like a football, he held it while I shoved the dressing in. Confronted with the problem of keeping the dressing in the bulging turkey, I used one of my darning needles, threaded with crochet cotton, to sew him up. Feeling like pros, we went to the Rice's house and repeated the process with their turkey, as I had plenty of dressing for that bird, too.

Jeanne and Ed stopped by our place Christmas Eve—Jeanne had left their children's gifts with me—and Dusty came right over and invited us all to their place. After several rounds of drinks, we put together the toys that the Leys had for their children, using the directions only when all else failed.

The assembled forts, filled with toy soldiers, knights, cannons, etc., were too much of a temptation. Ed decided to test the firing capability of one of the cannons. He aimed and fired. The trajectory was perfect and he slayed one of the toy soldiers. Dusty and I, seated on the floor, had to test our dexterity. What fun! I don't know who got the idea—our brains were a little muddled from so much liquor—to set up a battlefield with soldiers on one side and knights on the other. War was declared and a battle ensued between the two armies. After a few misdirected shots, a person was hit. Then we began shooting the plastic ammunition at each other, with plastic bullets and projectiles flying everywhere. It was asinine behavior for supposedly responsible adults, but so hilariously funny!

By the time we'd finished assembling (and playing) with the Ley's children's gifts, and we'd wrapped Bonnie's gifts, it was past midnight, so I started the turkey before I went to bed Christmas Eve.

Christmas morning we opened our gifts; and I rearranged the living room so we'd have room for the Leys and the three of us to sit around the table. The turkey was roasting beautifully, and its aroma was filling the house.

Jeanne and her family arrived about noon. We reminisced over cocktails, comparing the last lonesome Christmas with our happy, family-like one this year. My dinner turned out better than I'd expected, considering the inadequate conveniences and thanks for Jeanne's roaster and the electricity remaining on. I excused myself from the table to go prepare the dessert. Right after I'd spread the meringue on the lemon pies, I remembered I had no oven. The electric roaster was soaking to loosen the grease and gravy, so I couldn't use it. There was no solution, so I served the pie with raw meringue. Bill was disappointed with me and Ed teased me unmercifully, but we all ate the pie anyway.

The day after Christmas, when our house was in complete chaos from the aftermath of a Christmas dinner, wrapping strewn about and the clutter of taking down the Christmas decorations and tree, I could have clobbered Ed when he and Jeanne arrived with Ed's new boss, a full colonel and his wife, informing me they'd come for lunch!

Protocol was forgotten over cold turkey sandwiches and beer. I knew we were accepted when the colonel's wife asked me to call her by her first name and asked if she might accompany Jeanne and I on some of our excursions she'd heard about.

We'd spent a little over a year in Japan. The Leys had been like family. Although we were still in private rental, I finally had to admit to myself that I was beginning to enjoy life in Japan.

Part IV

Sayonara

61

After the holidays and the children were back in school, I started reading all I could find about places of interest in Japan. This would help us better plan our future sight-seeing trips. I wasn't going to be content to frequent only the American operated concessions and clubs as so many American dependents were prone to do. With the exception of a few inconveniences, that was much the same as living on a military base anywhere.

Then blood started appearing in my urine. At the dispensary, I told the doctor that during the last few days aboard ship my urine looked like rusty rain water. I hadn't mentioned it to anyone and it had cleared up after the boat trip. I'd suspected it was the result of drinking converted ocean water. I'd had no pain then nor did I now. The doctor prescribed some medication and a week later he suggested I go to the Tokyo Army General Hospital for tests.

The hospital was on the other side of Tokyo from our place. Luckily, Bill was able to drive me there. I was scheduled for an early morning X-ray. Stretched out on that hard X-ray table, my skinny bones rubbing on that hard, cold table and my mouth feeling like it was lined with cotton, in walked a WAC Medic.

"Good morning," she said. "Be with you in a minute. I can't do a thing until I've had my morning cup of coffee."

And she proceeded to pour herself a cup and sat there and drank it!

A doctor came in and explained they were going to insert some dye in my veins and take X-rays of my kidneys. He reprimanded the WAC Medic for drinking coffee in front of me, as I hadn't had any food or liquid for more than twelve hours. Then he instructed her on the importance of controlling the flow of dye into my veins and gave her the estimated amount of time it should take.

The WAC Medic must have resented the doctor's reprimand. She jammed that needle in my arm and started really pumping on the plunger. In a matter of seconds I felt nauseated and told her. She told me to breathe deeply and kept right on feeding in the dye. My mouth filled with soured saliva and when I opened it to ask her to get a pan for me, my stomach curled up into a tight knot and I vomited, going into violent dry heaves.

The doctor rushed in, shoved the WAC Medic aside and pulled the needle out of my arm. He really chewed her out, telling her she was giving the dye too fast. He wiped the perspiration from my face, and explained that using the dye was out of the question now so he'd have to use a cystoscope. I didn't know what he was talking about and, too weak to ask any questions, he proceeded working on me.

The pain was excruciating. I thought he'd never finish. It could have been only seconds, or it could have been an hour—I don't know. But I couldn't believe him when, after he'd finally finished, he said I could get dressed and go home. And then told me to come back in about two weeks and he'd give me the results of the X-rays.

Bill drove me home. Tears run down my face, dripping off of my nose and chin. I was still in a lot of pain, and I was so mad about the treatment I'd received.

A couple of weeks later when it was time to go back to the hospital and get the report of my X-rays, Jeanne wanted to go with me and see a dermatologist. We knew we'd probably never find the hospital by driving, so we took the bus.

The bus ride required many transfers and the rough ride was tiring.

The Army General Hospital was situated near a river or waterway. This section of Tokyo was appalling. How young some of the little homeless gamins were who had to beg or steal for a living, trying to survive in the squalor of back alleys and using large packing boxes or abandoned and over-turned rickshaws for shelter. I was amazed at the large number of families who lived on sampans or river boats. Perhaps all cities with waterways have similar conditions, but this was my first time of being in the midst of such a neighborhood, and it seemed poorer and more retched than anything I'd ever seen.

The doctor told me the X-rays showed that one kidney was a different shape than the other. He advised me to come back in a couple or three months and they'd take more X-rays to see if my kidneys were the same or had changed. The bleeding had stopped, and I decided I wasn't about to go through that torture again. The next time I went to that hospital they'd have to carry me in on a stretcher. However, Jeanne had better luck with her doctor.

Jeanne had to return to the hospital a second time. Ed drove her, and I went along just for the ride. Ed and I started walking along the waterway. We located a place where we could take a boat ride and tour the complete circle around Tokyo; but we resisted the temptation, as we didn't know how long it would take, and continued on foot.

Many of the boats, besides being homes, were fishermen's boats, loaded with their catch, or were in the business of transporting coal or other products. We watched as one poor old man unloaded coal by carrying it in little baskets hanging from an A-frame on his bent shoulders. It was a slow, hard process, to say the least.

This seemed to be the center of the fishing industry. Fish markets lined the narrow streets. Many wooden frames set up in the street contained fish drying in the sun and got a good dusting when vehicles sped down the road. Using a hypodermic needle, a Japanese man was injecting a colored dye in some fish—perhaps to give them the color of fresh fish, or possibly it was a preservative.

A little Japanese boy and girl started following us at a safe distance. Ed offered them some yen if they would let us take their picture. They posed for us, grinning from ear to ear, and then trotted along at our heels for the remainder of our hike, popping into every picture we took. Regular little pros in a con game. It was an interesting part of the city and we leisurely covered several blocks, taking many pictures, before returning to the hospital. Jeanne was impatiently waiting for us in the car, but later forgave us for being gone so long.

62

One afternoon in late January Jeanne knocked on my door and Bill followed her into the house. The minute I saw them I knew something was wrong. Jeanne told me to sit down, they had something to tell me. Bill had received a cable from the States that my brother had suffered a serious heart attack and my sister wanted me to come home. It didn't seem possible. It couldn't be. My brother was only forty-two. I felt utterly lost. He was clear around on the other side of the world and I felt so helpless.

Jeanne and Bill were discussing the time difference and the possibility that Paul (my brother) could be much better or, heaven forbid, was already gone. Jeanne suggested we call home and get a current report before deciding on anything. Bill placed a call to my sister and learned that Paul was critical and not expected to live. After trying to consider everything, we finally agreed that Bonnie and I should return to the States.

During the next two days the U.S. Embassy took care of getting our airplane reservations, we were each given a physical checkup, received our orders, had all our papers cleared and were ready to depart on Saturday.

Pappa-san, the tailor, made Bonnie a new coat from material I'd purchased, and when he delivered it he presented her with a matching hat he'd made as a farewell present. I only had about five dollars worth of yen, so Bill told Bonnie she could buy anything she wanted with it as a last memento of Japan. She headed straight for the silver shop where we'd shopped, told the owner she wanted a charm bracelet and showed him her yen. He told her to pick out the charms she wanted and he'd tell her when she'd spent all her money. Selecting the bracelet and charms she wanted, he attached the charms and then added one more as his present to her—a real pearl enclosed in a little bird cage. He was very generous, because her bracelet was loaded with charms and I'm sure their value totaled more than five dollars.

On the way to the airport we stopped at Ley's for a final goodbye. Ed fixed me a stiff drink to calm my nerves, and Bill asked Jeanne if she would help him sort out our furniture for shipment back to the States. Rushing on to the airport, we stopped and exchanged my Military Pay Script for American dollars, then to the terminal to check our luggage.

It was difficult trying to say goodbye to Bill. Our names were being broadcast over the loud speaker that the plane was ready to take off, so there wasn't time for a long, emotional goodbye.

The air terminal and airline employees were most helpful to Bonnie and me. We were royally escorted to the plane where the steward and stewardess met us and directed us to our seats. The only other passengers on the flight were traveling tourist class, so we had the whole tail section to ourselves.

As the plane climbed and circled over Tokyo, heading east, the lights of the city began blinking on and each new light released another tear until my cheeks were drenched as the tears spilled out of my eyes. My heart felt like it was being torn in two, half of it going home and half of it staying in Japan.

It grew dark rapidly, flying away from the sun. We were served a delicious dinner (with champagne for me), after which

I was briefed on how to operate the life jackets (I'm glad we didn't have to use them, because their directions went in one ear and out the other).

I had trouble settling down. The last two days had been horrendous with little sleep and so many decisions, plans and arrangements to be made under such sorrowful circumstances. The reason I was going home was sad enough, but on top of that I had to leave Bill, and we would have been moving into the new quarters in another week or two. And Ed and Jeanne—when, if ever, would I see them again? It was unbelievable that we'd become such close friends, like family. We'd been together every day for over a year, yet never once had there been any arguments, hard feelings or jealousy between us. Friends like that are rare.

Then I remembered the time I'd rearranged all of Jeanne's furniture, the day after Ed had broken his arm, and he'd fallen over an end table going to the kitchen in the dark—it's a wonder he didn't break his other arm, or mine! And the night Bill and Ed spliced the movie film, putting all the little reels together into a big reel, each gulping a drink between reels. When the splicing was finished, they ran the film through the projector and the pictures all ran backwards on the screen. Jeanne and I were laughing so hard as we were trying to tell them they had to rewind the film first. In their drunken stupor, they didn't believe us, turned the roll over and then the film not only went backwards but the pictures were upside down; and we almost collapsed with hysteria when they unwound over a hundred feet of movie film all over the floor in order to rewind it. And dear little Roddie, so wise for his young years, telling me not to worry if we had to bail out of the plane because the life jackets would keep us afloat. Then thoughtfully added that the water would probably be pretty cold.

These happy thoughts brought back other pleasant memories and, mixed with the liquor, I relaxed and drifted off to sleep.

The stewardess gently shook my shoulders to awaken me and tell me we would soon be landing on Shimia Island, one of the Aleutians. It was still quite dark outside but I could see the airport lights outlining the runway. It didn't look large enough for our Turbo Jet DC to land on, but the pilot brought us down safe and sound. This stop was for refueling and all passengers were asked to leave the plane as the motors and heat would be turned off.

This would be my first chance to get a really good, deep breath of fresh air instead of the "smit" of Tokyo. (Jeanne had come up with that—like, New York's "smaze" and San Francisco's "smog.") Stepping outside the plane, I inhaled deeply. What a surprise—my nostrils froze together! Then, through the dark, I could see the mechanics had on fur-lined parkas and fur-lined gloves; and although I couldn't hear them, I could see their words floating through the air.

Bonnie and I lost no time in running down the steps and to the waiting room where it was warm. It was about ten o'clock in the morning, and the temperature was forty degrees below zero. We chatted with some of our fellow passengers as we snacked on the fresh fruit, fruit juices, sweet rolls and coffee furnished by the airline.

Then we were on to Alaska, where the sun greeted us as we neared Anchorage. The snow-covered mountains sparkled like diamonds, and the ocean looked like it had large soap flakes floating on it. As we zoomed along the runway, we saw a big bull moose dart into the woods.

We were all fumigated before leaving the plane, and then were checked through customs. The inspectors asked us a few questions and then peeked in my luggage. Since I'd packed hurriedly, when the upside down bag was opened, all my underclothes fell out! The inspectors grinned and waved us through as, red-faced, I shoved my undies back in the bag.

Again, the airlines furnished a special room and a selection of food. After a quick bite, we toured the terminal. At a souvenir shop we added an ivory penguin to Bonnie's charm bracelet. When I paid for it, I knew we were back in the States. This one charm cost as much as her bracelet and other charms together.

We took a walk outside through the snow, even though it was bitter cold it was more brisk than penetrating, and Bonnie enjoyed crawling up an eight-foot snow bank and sliding down.

Our flight took us on to Seattle where the night closed in on us, made even darker by dark clouds and rain. The air terminal was quite large with lots of interesting stateside things to see, but we headed straight for the restaurant and ordered chocolate milkshakes. Oh, how good that fresh milk did taste. We transferred to another plane for a non-stop flight to Chicago, and I dropped off to sleep again.

I awoke to the most beautiful sunrise I'd ever seen. Flying high above a solid mass of clouds, the sunlight transformed them into ever-changing colors: from dark blues, reds, purples, and golds; fading into light blues, lavenders, pinks and yellow; and finally into dazzling whites edged with just a hint of pastels, making them look like globs of luscious whipped cream. It was more beautiful than words could ever portray—surely a sneak preview of what heaven must be like.

Our plane landed in Chicago at six o'clock on Sunday morning. Was this really possible? We'd left Tokyo at six p.m. Saturday evening. However, we'd crossed the International Dateline and, in reality, had been flying backwards in time, as Japan is nineteen hours ahead of Illinois time.

The train ride from Chicago to Champaign, Illinois, closed an interesting and enlightening chapter of my life. So many experiences that could never be relived nor recreated because circumstances, people and places change and, without a written account, memory could become dimmed and distorted with the passing of time. I promised myself that somehow I'd get that written account down on paper before the experience passed out of my mind.

But more important for my own frame of mind were the lessons I'd learned. Although I'd only scratched the surface in learning about Japan and her people, it was sufficient to convince me that my preconceived ideas about them were all wrong. I'd come to believe that Americans should have a deep, sincere respect for their traditions and heritage, as well as all people of our world, regardless of their race or religion, and try to understand our fellow men before we judge them. And I'd come to realize more than I ever had before that we Americans who are fortunate enough to travel to a foreign country should remember that we are, in fact, ambassadors whose friendliness, courtesy, appearance and conduct, more than words, portray the American life.

After two more weeks in intensive care, followed by several weeks of uncertainty, wondering whether my brother was going to pull through, he started coming around and recovered from his heart attack and regained his health. He lived another eighteen years.

Bill decided he didn't want to serve the remainder of his tour of duty in Japan without us and submitted his unconditional resignation. It was granted and he returned to California, where he received an honorable discharge in April 1956. He re-enlisted for Chanute Air Force Base and returned to Rantoul, Illinois, where we built a home that fall and continued to reside after his retirement from the Air Force.